Bibliometrics and Research Evaluation

History and Foundations of Information Science
Edited by Michael Buckland, Jonathan Furner, and Markus Krajewski

Bibliometrics and Research Evaluation

Uses and Abuses

Yves Gingras

The MIT Press
Cambridge, Massachusetts
London, England

This book was set in Stone Sans and Stone Serif by Toppan Best-set Premedia Limited. Printed and bound in the United States of America.

Library of Congress Cataloging-in-Publication Data

Names: Gingras, Yves, 1954- author.
Title: Bibliometrics and research evaluation : uses and abuses / Yves Gingras.
Other titles: Dérives de l'évaluation de la recherche. English
Description: Cambridge, MA : The MIT Press, [2016] | Series: History and
    foundations of information science | Includes bibliographical references
    and index.
Identifiers: LCCN 2016014090 | ISBN 9780262035125 (hardcover : alk. paper)
Subjects: LCSH: Bibliometrics. | Research--Evaluation. | Education,
    Higher--Research--Evaluation. | Universities and colleges--Research--Evaluation.
Classification: LCC Q180.55.E9 G5613 2016 | DDC 020.72/7--dc23 LC record
    available at https://lccn.loc.gov/2016014090

10 9 8 7 6 5 4 3 2 1

Contents

Introduction

Since the first decade of the new millennium, the words *ranking, evalua-*
tion, metrics, h-index, and *impact factors* have wreaked havoc in the world
of higher education and research.[1] Governments and research administrators want to evaluate everything—teachers, professors, researchers, training
programs, and universities—using quantitative indicators. This demand,
which has its roots in the ideology of the "New Public Management" of the
1980s, led to the multiplication of indicators of *excellence* and *quality,* terms
often used with little concern for their exact meaning and validity.[2]

Among the tools used to measure "research excellence," pride of place
has been given to *bibliometrics*, a research specialty that typically analyzes
the number of scientific publications produced by a given entity (individual, institution, country, what have you) and the number of citations
that they receive. While the number of papers provides a simple indicator
of production (and productivity, if a time unit is defined), the number of
citations that a paper receives is often considered an intuitive measure of
the quality and scientific impact of the published research. Used to rank
universities, laboratories, and researchers, various combinations of these
numbers provide indicators that are considered an "objective" measure of
the value of research results that—many argue—should usefully replace the
more "subjective" evaluations that have been in use since the seventeenth
century.

Confronted with the generalized use of quantitative indicators to evaluate their research activities, many scientists thus discovered bibliometrics
in the 1990s and started to criticize its use, denouncing its shortcomings
and the perverse effects that these simplistic indicators may have on the
dynamics of scientific research. However, and paradoxically, researchers
themselves are often the first to highlight the impact factor of the journals

in which they publish and to display their total number of citations or their h-index (more on this to come later) as signs of their own value and success, without always understanding the real meaning and validity of such indicators. Also, they often do not hesitate, as members of evaluation committees, to use these same measures to rank their colleagues and decide whether they should get research grants. Thus, one cannot seriously blame only the bureaucrats for the onset of the "bibliometric fever" that emerged in the 1990s and generated the proliferation of rankings that excited many university presidents despite the fact—as we shall argue in this book—that these rankings have no real scientific validity and rarely measure what they say they do.

Although the use of bibliometric data is rarely the only kind of information used in the various rankings and evaluations, its sudden discovery by scientists has promoted the false and unfortunate equation that bibliometrics = evaluation, as if it had no other uses outside the evaluation game. It is, in fact, a lack of serious methodological reflection that has led to the anarchic use of bibliometric indicators in research evaluation. In spite of the countless letters complaining about the abuses of various bibliometric indicators and university rankings that have been published by scientists in *Nature* and *Science* or on blogs, most criticisms to date have only focused on underlining the supposed limits of bibliometric indicators, thus taking for granted that they provide otherwise valid measures. Critics rarely question the epistemological foundations of these indicators: Do they have the meaning that is attributed to them? Do they measure what they are supposed to measure? Are they appropriate to the concepts that they are supposed to measure (quality, productivity, impact, etc.)?

The problems raised by the abundant, though largely redundant[3], literature on the abuses of bibliometrics in research evaluation are often the result of the ill-defined relation between a concept and its indicators, as well as the lack of specification of the scale at which the indicators are valid (if so) and useful. Given that it is impossible (not to say undesirable) to escape evaluation altogether, it is crucial to understand the specific properties of the most common bibliometric indicators and rigorously criticize the ones that are poorly constructed and whose use could cause (or have already caused) unintended negative consequences. This task is even more urgent when one learns that 70% of higher education managers of European universities admit using published university rankings to make policy decisions, even though, as we shall see, it has been shown many times that the measures used in these rankings are invalid and that, in fact, only about 15% of international students know of the existence of these rankings, and only 10% of the latter use them to choose a university.[4]

The main objective of this book, therefore, is to present in a succinct manner the basic concepts and methods of bibliometrics in order to demonstrate that they have a much broader scope than just research evaluation, which is a relatively recent (and unwise) application of its methods. In chapter 1, I review the origins of bibliometrics as a research domain and show how its uses moved, roughly, from library management in the 1950s and 1960s to science policy in the 1970s, and finally to research evaluation in the 1980s. The next three chapters then focus in turn on the good, the bad, and the ugly uses of bibliometric indicators and rankings.

Focusing first on the good uses, chapter 2 shows that the study of publication and citation patterns, on the proper scale, provides a unique tool for analyzing the global dynamics of science over time. Along the way, many myths still circulating among scientists about publications and citations are shown to have no empirical basis and be just that—myths. In chapter 3, I demonstrate that the evaluation of research is a very ancient practice, beginning with the emergence of scientific papers in the mid-seventeenth century, and that new layers have been added during the twentieth century to include the evaluation of grants, graduate programs, research laboratories, and even universities as a whole. All these evaluations were essentially qualitative and based on peer review committees until the 1980s, when bibliometric indicators began to be more systematically used to add a quantitative approach, which was perceived to be more objective than the more traditional qualitative approach, now considered too subjective to be taken seriously according to positivist conceptions of "decision making."

Not surprisingly, the more these quantitative indicators became entrenched in the formal evaluation procedures of institutions and researchers, the more likely they gave rise to abuses. In chapters 3 and 4, I thus analyze the bad uses of ill-defined quantitative indicators—the ones that often generate perverse and unintended effects on the dynamic of research—as well as the even uglier ones, consisting of manipulating the data or even paying authors to add new addresses to their papers in order to boost the position of certain institutions on the many competing world rankings of universities. I also consider questions that rarely have been raised by promoters, as well as critics of bibliometric indicators, such as: Why do the so-called journal impact factors go to three decimal places? And who really needs them to know the quality of a journal article? In other words, I pay attention to the politics of evaluation and show that using numbers is also a way to control scientists and diminish their autonomy in the evaluation process.

In order to contribute to better quality control of the various bibliometric indicators circulating in the now-booming evaluation market, the final chapter analyzes the sources of data used and their limitations, and proposes precise criteria for establishing the validity of indicators at a given scale of analysis (e.g., individuals, institutions, or countries). It also tries to understand why so many university managers adapt their practices and policies based on their positions in rankings that in turn are based on flawed measures of research quality. In conclusion, I suggest that by being too eager to let invalid indicators influence their research strategies, universities are in fact echoing the old story "The Emperor's New Clothes."

This book is an opinionated essay, not a survey of the huge (and, as I have said, often redundant and superficial) bibliometric literature devoted to the various aspects of research evaluation. Endnotes point the reader to many specific papers but cannot refer to all of them. My selection of what to highlight is based on what I consider the best contributions to the questions I discuss. It will be easy for those who want to know more about a specific detail to find appropriate sources by starting there or perusing journals like *Scientometrics, Journal of Informetrics, JASIST, Science and Public Policy,* and *Research Evaluation,* to name the major ones, as well as the recent book *Beyond Bibliometrics,* edited by Blaise Cronin and Cassidy R. Sugimoto.[5]

In his extensive review of the French version of this book, now revised and updated, my colleague Michel Zitt refers to more than fifty specialized papers that develop aspects of the many questions that I discuss here.[6] This gives me the opportunity to note explicitly what was implicit in the original French edition: the book is aimed at researchers and managers of research and other participants in higher education who are confronted with bibliometrics in their work, and I hope the brevity and tone of this contribution will make it readable. Seasoned experts in bibliometrics will not learn much about technical matters (except maybe my criteria for testing the validity of indicators).

Zitt concludes his generous review by noting that I offer a "committed vision, albeit one without nuances."[7] Readers will judge for themselves the level of "nuances" I offer, but I think that drowning readers in too many technical details may lead to missing the message and the important question: Why is there still so much confusion among scientists and university presidents, administrators, and managers about the basic concepts and indicators based on bibliometrics, even though thousands of specialized papers have been published on this topic over the last fifty years? One explanation could be that too many bibliometricians have focused exclusively on the intricacies of counting any units they could find (citations, tweets, views, Web connections, etc.), instead of asking first: What is the *meaning* of those measures? To paraphrase the formulation of a researcher who analyzed the Programme for International Student Assessment (PISA) test of literacy produced by the Organisation for Economic Co-operation and Development (OECD): the metric is the answer, but what is the question?[8]

I thus hope that by focusing on the basic questions of evaluations and their effects on scientific research—as opposed to the technical debate surrounding the proper way to calibrate a specific indicator—this little book will provide users of bibliometric evaluation, as well as those who are evaluated, with conceptual tools to help them better evaluate the many indicators filling the "black boxes" of rankings that are now for sale on the new market of research evaluation.

Acknowledgments

The original French version of this book owes its existence to an invitation for me to deliver a lecture on bibliometrics at the Institut National de la Recherche Agronomique (INRA) in Paris in June 2011. This event convinced me it was time to take stock of multiple and often wrongheaded debates on bibliometrics in relation to research evaluation. Having been involved in many bibliometric evaluations, and having talked many times in various forums over the past twenty years, I thought it would be useful to provide a more comprehensive picture of the good, bad, and ugly uses—and abuses— of bibliometrics in research evaluation.[9] I want to thank my colleagues who reviewed the text and made helpful suggestions: first, my longtime close collaborator Vincent Larivière, Jérôme Bourdieu, Michel Grossetti, Johan Heilbron, Camille Limoges, Franck Poupeau, Wiktor Stoczkowski, and

Jean-Philippe Warren. Also, thanks to Jean-Philippe Robitaille and Pierre Mongeon for the preparation of the figures, to Pauline Huet for formatting the endnotes, and to Eugene Garfield for the permission to use figures 2.1 and 2.12 and Katy Börner and Kevin Boyack for figure 2.13. I remain, of course, solely responsible for any remaining errors or infelicities the book may still contain. I have translated, revised, and updated it for this English edition, taking into accounts comments and suggestions made by reviewers of the original French version, as well as by two anonymous readers chosen by MIT Press. A particular thanks to Jean-François Blanchette, who thought that an English translation would be useful and made first contact with MIT Press on the subject of publishing it, to my colleague, Peter Keating, who carefully read the final text; and to Gita Devi Manaktala, for her wonderful and efficient support during all the process from translation to publication. Finally, thanks to Monique Dumont who prepared the index.

1   The Origins of Bibliometrics

Before beginning this discussion of bibliometrics, let us clarify the terminology of the field. The term *scientometrics,* generally attributed to the physicist Vassily Vassilievich Nalimov (who used its Russian equivalent, *naukometriya,* in the title of a book published in 1969), covers the quantitative measurement of all kinds of scientific activities, in all disciplines.[1] Its data include the amount of money invested in research and development (R&D), the scientific personnel involved in R&D, and the production of articles and patents. *Bibliometrics,* a term coined in 1969 by Alan Pritchard, is thus a subset of scientometrics, and it is limited to the analysis of publications and their properties.[2] When the analysis of patents is involved, the term *technometrics* is often used.

Although we tend to think of scientific *articles* in this field, publications include other kinds of documents as well, including (at least in principle) books, PhD theses, and the so-called gray literature of research reports. The more or less sophisticated analysis of these various kinds of publications essentially depends on their availability in the form of databases. Before computers made possible the automatic processing of large amounts of data, bibliometric data were gathered manually and covered only a relatively small number of publications (i.e., several dozen) pertaining to specific disciplines such as chemistry and sociology. With the advent of the Internet, the term *webometrics* has been added to the vocabulary to cover the analysis of the electronic access and use of scientific publications. Despite these formal distinctions, the terms *scientometrics* and *bibliometrics* have rapidly become interchangeable as the analysis of scientific production (whether in paper or electronic form) came to occupy a central position in the study of the dynamics of science.[3]

Citation Analysis as a Journal Collection Management Tool

The conventional birth of bibliometrics is usually associated with the publication in the mid-1920s of a now-classic study of the distribution of researchers' scientific productivity by the American statistician Alfred Lotka. In this seminal paper, Lotka establishes the law that now bears his name, which states that the number of authors P who publish N articles is inversely proportional to the square of N.[4] However, as Benoît Godin has shown, psychologists were in fact the first, in the early twentieth century, to analyze the evolution of the number of publications in their field, thus doing bibliometrics without using that word.[5] Other scientists also analyzed the evolution of the number of publications over time to trace the history of their discipline.[6] But contrary to Lotka's works, these analyses were not intended to find general laws; rather, they aimed only to track the growth of their own specialty.

Despite these early examples, bibliometric studies only started to become more systematic with the development, during the 1920s and 1930s, of the management of library journal collections. As academic journals increased in number and cost, librarians have sought objective methods to select the ones that were the most useful to researchers. In this context of journal collection management, citation analysis really took off. Instead of just counting publications, librarians started looking at the references (i.e., citations) that they contained to measure how useful papers and journals were in fact to scientists. By analyzing which journals were the most cited in a given discipline (and over what period of time)—chemistry being the most studied area at first—librarians could separate those that were still useful from the ones that could be considered obsolete because they were rarely cited, and thus move them to make space for recent issues.

A study published in the journal *Science* in 1927 showed that instead of choosing the journals on the basis of the subjective interest of some researchers, it was better to find an objective and broader measure to determine their actual usefulness. Analyzing the content of the main U.S. chemistry journals for the year 1926, the authors, two chemists, found that although more than 247 different journals were cited, a majority (more than 130) got fewer than three citations.[7] Highlighting the prevalence of German journals, another chemist later noted the importance for young chemists to master the German language.[8] As a sign of the radical changes brought about by World War II, a study of citations in chemical engineering journals published in the mid-1950s observed a severe decline of citations to German journals by American chemists.[9]

Similar descriptive analyses of the references contained in scientific papers, based on limited samples, were also carried out in the humanities and social sciences.[10] They clearly show that many years before the American linguist Eugene Garfield promoted the idea of a "citation index" in the mid-1950s, scientists already understood intuitively that the citations contained in scientific papers provide useful information on the research practices of scientists and the social dynamics of science. The fact that German journals are much cited, the suggestion that students should thus learn German, and the observation of the lack of citations for many years to a journal that cost the library precious money that could be better invested, are findings would have been hard to reach through means other than citation analysis.

The growth of bibliometric analyses of different disciplines and specialties naturally led to the creation of concepts that were specific to this new research domain. To formalize the idea that a typical article has become less and less used (and thus cited) over time, the concept of a *half-life* of scientific literature, analogous with the radioactive decay of elements, was defined in the early 1960s. Analyzing the distribution of the age of references contained in articles and journals shows that it follows an exponential decay curve. By analogy, one can define a kind of half-life by counting the number of years it takes to cover 50% of the total number of references. This simple indicator provides a measure of the useful life of the scientific literature in a given field. For example, one can compare disciplines and see that history refers to documents older than twenty years more often than chemistry does (figure 1.1a). Early studies also showed that in mathematics, half of the cited publications are less than ten years old, whereas in physics, the half-life is shorter, at five years. This finding reveals the fact that mathematics items typically have, on average, a longer life than physics items.[11] Similarly, but with a forward-looking orientation, one can define the half-life of citations as the time it takes to accumulate half of the total number of citations received (figure 1.1b).

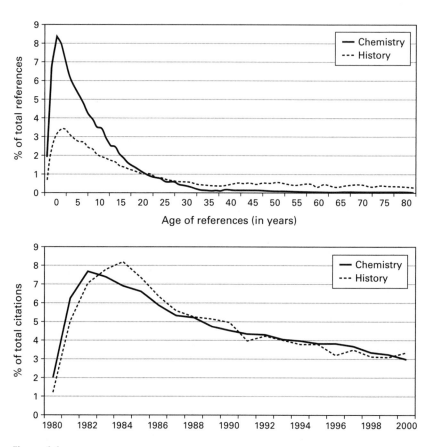

Figure 1.1
(a) Typical temporal distribution of the age of references contained in chemistry and history articles published in 1980; (b) typical temporal evolution of citations received by a group of chemistry and history papers in the years following their publication in 1980 (normalized to 100% of total citations)

The Science Citation Index: Automating Bibliographic Research

After World War II, the exponential growth in the number of articles published made it impossible for researchers to track the results of new research, even when limited to their own specialized area. The publication by private firms or learned societies of summaries of recent publications was no longer sufficient to accomplish the task. In 1946, the Royal Society of London organized two international conferences on scientific information, with the objective of improving "existing methods of collection, indexing, and distribution of scientific literature," and extending "existing abstracting services."[12] By the end of the 1940s, the problem of indexing all this literature in a manner that made it easy for scientists to find what they needed was obvious to all.

In this context, Eugene Garfield proposed in 1955 a plan to index all articles cited in the scientific literature. The model was based on *Shepard's Citations,* an index that listed all citations to legal decisions in the United States, making it easier to tell whether a given judgment was often referred to and possibly creating jurisprudence as well. Garfield first suggested to William C. Adair, then vice president of the Frank Shepard Company, the firm that produced this indispensable index for lawyers, to publish an article in the journal *American Documentation* describing the mode of operation of this legal tool and how it could be adapted to scientific literature.[13]

A few months after this article came out, Garfield published in the journal *Science* details of his own project: an electronic database of citations to the scientific literature.[14] The objective was to facilitate bibliographic research by using cited articles to help identify papers dealing with the same subject. The basic underlying intuition was that a citation to a given paper would suggest a conceptual link between the citing and the cited items. Finding new articles citing a particular paper of interest quickly build a relevant bibliography for it is quite plausible that an article that cites, for instance, Albert Einstein's 1905 paper on relativity theory is indeed concerned with that topic and not with chemistry. Similarly, finding papers that cite one's work allows one to read papers and find authors working on the same subject, and that may not necessarily be accomplished as simply by perusing the usual scientific journals.

Convinced of the usefulness and profitability of the project, Garfield founded the Institute for Scientific Information (ISI) in Philadelphia in 1959. In 1961, he received $300,000 from the National Science Foundation (NSF) and National Institutes of Health (NIH) to study the feasibility of an automated citation index. Once the prototype was developed, the ISI released the Science Citation Index (SCI) for 1963 and continued to expand its coverage over the years. The participation of NSF and NIH in the project indicated the importance that scientific organizations attached to the issue of access to scientific literature in a context of exponential information production.[15]

Having become the primary tool for evaluating the impact of scientific publications only in the 1980s, the SCI has emerged in the context of management of the scientific literature with no direct connection with research evaluation—a theme that, in the 1960s, was not yet on the agenda of organizations like NSF or NIH, let alone universities or governments. SCI, then, was primarily a bibliographic research tool that allowed scientists to find among the flood of publications the ones that interested them on a given subject. Even today, the Web of Science (WoS) and its recent competitor, Elsevier's Scopus database, provide unique tools that can construct a bibliography quickly on a given subject. Note that researchers keep calling them "indexes" because from the 1960s to the 1980s, the product was in fact a book that listed in alphabetical order the names of cited authors (see figure 2.1 in the next chapter). Information technologies have since transformed this paper index into an electronic database containing bibliographic references of the articles identified, which can be searched on the Internet, but the term *citation index* remains in use.

Bibliometrics for Science Policy

Derek de Solla Price, an English historian of science, gave scientometrics its first theoretical basis. A physicist by training, he proposed to analyze science as a collective phenomenon analogous with the statistical physics of a gas, following the evolution of all scientists and their publications rather than merely focusing on a single scientist, such as Albert Einstein. Price wanted to create what he called a "science of science" based on the quantitative analysis of scientific development. In 1950, he published a study showing that science as a system had grown exponentially since about 1700, with the number of both journals and publications doubling about every fifteen years.[16] Though the precise growth rate varies according to the method and data used, the exponential growth of science is a fact that has been confirmed by several studies.[17] Price was also the first to use the new SCI for sociological rather than bibliographic analysis. In an article on citation networks published in 1965, he highlighted the very uneven distribution of citations, which followed a power law similar to that of Lotka for the distribution of the productivity of researchers.[18]

Despite the work of librarians on citation analysis and the promotion of a science of science by Price, research in bibliometrics long remained confined to a small community composed of scientists, librarians, sociologists, and historians, who examined, each for their own reasons, the properties of scientific publications and of the references they contain (i.e., the citations). The real development of bibliometrics as an academic research field occurred only in the 1970s with the coming of age of science policy.

To understand why, recall that the second half of 1960 marked a turning point in the organization of science, as many countries showed a renewed interest in science policy and planning. Reflection on the ways to stimulate the development of research required indicators of research and innovation, much as economic and social development indicators were designed in the wake of the economic crisis of the 1930s and World War II.[19] The Organisation for Economic Co-operation and Development (OECD) thus launched a series of studies on national science policies. In 1962, the agency published the first edition of the *Frascati Manual*, which offers convenient standard definitions for the measurement of research and development.[20] In 1965, Price published an article in *Nature* on "the scientific foundations of science policy."[21]

It was in this context that the NSF (which, as discussed previously, helped Garfield create the SCI) was mandated by the U.S. Congress to produce a series of indicators to monitor and measure the status of American science and technology. This led to the publication in 1972 of the first biennial volume of *Science Indicators*. Adapting its content to changing policies, *Science Indicators* became *Science and Engineering Indicators* in 1987. Again in the early 1970s, NSF asked Francis Narin and his firm, Computer Horizons, to study the possibility of using bibliometrics for evaluation purposes. Narin produced a lengthy report that laid the foundations of evaluative bibliometrics.[22]

While the OECD, mainly driven by an economic vision of scientific development, remained primarily interested in input and patent indicators (the latter used as a measure of innovation), NSF, closer to the academic world, sought indicators on publications and their impact—the kind of data that the SCI could now provide. Thus, for the first time, data on publications and citations were included in a set of science and innovation indicators in addition to the more usual data on the scientific workforce and levels of R & D investments. These data sets served as a model for other countries, which from the mid-1980s also started to use bibliometric data to monitor their level of scientific development.[23]

Government demand for indicators capable of measuring the level of scientific and technological development, and thereby provide the necessary information to design national science and technological policies, stimulated the development of a previously dispersed research domain and led to the creation in 1971 of the journal *Research Policy*, followed two years later by *Science and Public Policy*. These journals were especially devoted to the analysis of the social and economic factors affecting the development of science and technology in different countries. In 1974, a conference was convened where the pioneers of bibliometrics reflected on the theme "Toward a Metric of Science: The Advent of the Science Indicators."[24] The historical, sociological, and economic aspects of the measurement of science were analyzed by various experts with the aim of producing a coherent model for the development of science indicators. Gerald Holton, a physics professor and historian of science at the conference, wondered aloud if science could really be measured, while other sociologists, the brothers Stephen and Jonathan Cole, discussed the cognitive aspects of scientific disciplines. For their part, Garfield and his colleagues showed that quantitative methods such as bibliographic coupling and co-citation analysis of documents could be used as a tool for mapping the conceptual structure of scientific disciplines and specialties, as well as their temporal development.[25]

The next chapter will discuss the different uses of these bibliometric methods and indicators. For now, it suffices to note that the growth of bibliometric research led to the usual trappings of a scientific discipline—that is journals, congresses, and learned societies. The first journal devoted entirely to this topic, *Scientometrics*, was created in 1978; ten years later, in 1987, an annual international congress started to convene, and in 1993, a learned society was founded called the International Society for Scientometrics and Informetrics. The very existence of the computerized database of the SCI also encouraged research projects using bibliometric data. The 1970s saw the development of the sociology of science as a specialty, with its own journal, *Social Studies of Science*, established in 1971, in which several studies using bibliometric data to analyze the development of scientific disciplines were published.

Bibliometrics for Research Evaluation

Having been used mainly in the management of library collections of journals and as a source of data for academic research on the development of science, bibliometric tools began to be used for evaluating the productivity and scientific impact of research activities in the 1980s. Indicator-based management methods, first applied in the private sector and based on the ideas of benchmarking and knowledge management, were transferred to the public sector in the 1980s and to universities in the 1990s.[26] In search of productivity and performance indicators adapted to the evaluation of academic activities, the managers of higher education saw in bibliometric data the tools they needed to construct indicators that would go beyond the traditional peer review, which was increasingly perceived as too subjective and in need to be complemented, if not replaced, by data considered more objective. Created in 1991, the journal *Research Evaluation* reflected this turn toward research management and continues to publish results on research assessments often based on bibliometric indicators.

Until the start of the twenty-first century, most bibliometric analysis was done at the level of countries, universities, or laboratories, not to assess individuals. Most experts are indeed wary of the application of bibliometric measures at the individual level, given the nature of bibliometric data and the large fluctuations of the numbers at such a microscale. Despite warnings by many scientometricians, the practice of using bibliometric indicators to evaluate individual scientists has developed among managers and researchers improvising as experts in evaluation. This uncritical and undisciplined (and often invalid) use of bibliometric indicators has been facilitated by the fact that bibliographic databases now can be accessed easily through university libraries (i.e., Scopus and the WoS) and the Internet (i.e., Google Scholar). Today, scientists can play with publication and citation numbers without much regard for the meaning of the data, doing what I call "wild bibliometrics" (analogous to Freud's denunciation of "wild psychoanalysis"), which gives rise to inadequate and invalid indicators like the h-index, as will be discussed in the following chapters of this book.

To summarize, from the 1920s until the late 1950s, bibliometrics relied on manual methods, was limited to small samples, and was used primarily to help manage journal collections in libraries. The computerized database of the SCI opened the way, in the early 1960s, to large-scale analyses of the dynamics of scientific change. This innovation also came at a time when science policy was emerging and needed new indicators to measure the global level of scientific development of countries. During the 1970s and 1980s, this situation fostered the study of the dynamics of science across disciplines and specialties, as well as on the national and international levels.

Since the 1990s, bibliometrics has become a central tool for the evaluation of research and researchers. Subject to these new quantitative evaluation methods, researchers suddenly discovered bibliometrics, which they naturally (and mechanically) associate with evaluation. Many react negatively to this simplistic quantification of their research activities and criticize the limitations of the indicators and data used, rediscovering weaknesses long known to experts in the field. Other less critical scientists have used the opportunity to invent new indicators by combining, in a more or less fanciful manner, bibliometric data on papers and citations, even forging equations to identify the best researchers. These abuses of evaluative bibliometrics have discredited a set of methods that are nonetheless essential for those who want to understand the global dynamics of science.

Interestingly, whereas papers produced by experts in bibliometrics tend to appear in specialized journals, those produced by scientists since the 1990s tend to be published in their own disciplinary journals and often consist in listings of the most-cited authors or journals in their fields. Being peer-reviewed by colleagues who are not themselves knowledgeable in bibliometrics, they are published even when the work ignores the existing specialized literature on the subject. It must also be said, finally, that too many publications in bibliometrics do not take into account the sociological aspects of the dynamics of science, thus talking about "citations" and "tweets" and "blogs" as if they were on the same level and responded to the same sociological dynamics. In order to go beyond the false equation bibliometrics = evaluation, the next chapter will recall what kind of results can be obtained about the social dynamics of science on a global scale from the rational use of bibliometric data.

2 What Bibliometrics Teaches Us about the Dynamics of Science

As discussed in the previous chapter, the rapid expansion of bibliometric analysis depended on having access to an electronic database that made data analysis on a large scale possible. For about forty years, starting in 1963, the only source of bibliometric data was Eugene Garfield's Science Citation Index (SCI), produced by his company, the Institute for Scientific Information (ISI). We had to wait until 2004 for a competing database, Scopus, produced by Elsevier. This long monopoly explains why all the publications in the field of scientometrics were until recently based on the ISI databases. Studies based on the Scopus database, however, have multiplied in recent years. A third source of bibliometric information, Google Scholar, also appeared on the scene during the 2000s, but it does not have the same neat structure as the other two, which provide organized information on addresses and countries of authors, as well as the list of references (citations) in their papers, a classification into subfields, and other resources, thus facilitating the analysis of publications and citations at the level of institutions and countries.

The Content of a Citation Index

Let us look at the basic structure of the SCI database, now integrated into the Thomson Reuters Web of Science (WoS). ISI published the SCI first, to which were added the Social Science Citation Index (SSCI), and the Arts and Humanities Citation Index (AHCI) in 1973 and 1978, respectively. Before the Internet became the norm, they were available only in subscribing university libraries as large volumes resembling telephone books, and then, as of the 1980s, in the form of compact discs. It goes without saying that the paper form did not lend itself to comprehensive analyses, and the

```
EINSTEIN A--------*05*ANN PHYSIK----------      17   549
        KING AL          BIOC BIOP A      60     42   344
        ROSSI C          NATURE           61    189   822
    ----------------06-ANN PHYSIK----------      19   289
        ELWORTHY PH      J CHEM SOC       59          1951
        VARADAIAH VV     J POLYM SCI      60     46   528
        WHITNAH CH       J DAIRY SCI      59     42   227
    ----------------06-ANN PHYSIK----------      19   371
        KING AL          BIOC BIOP A      60     42   344
    ----------------07-JAHRB RADIOAKT ELEKT       4   411
        DEBEAURE. O      COMPT REND       60    250  2149
    ----------------08-ANN PHYSIK----------      25   205
        FIXMAN M         J CHEM PHYS      60     33  1357
    ----------------08-Z ELEKTROCHEM-------      14   235
        MAJUMDAR SK      NATURWISSEN      60     47    39
    ----------------10-ANN PHYSIK----------      33  1275
        BULLOUGH RK      J POLYM SCI      60     46   517
        COUMOU DJ        J COLL SCI       60     15   408
    ----------------11-ANN PHYSIK----------      34   591
        ELWORTHY PH      J CHEM SOC       59          1951
        GIBBONS RA       BIOCHEM J        59     73   217
        VARADAIAH VV     J POLYM SCI      60     46   528
    ----------------12-ANN PHYSIK----------      38   355
        WHITROW GJ       NATURE           60    188   790
    ----------------12-ANN PHYSIK----------      38   443
        WHITROW GJ       NATURE           60    188   790
    ----------------24-Z PHYSIK----------      27     1
        BAKANOV SP       DISC FARAD       60          130
    ----------------26-INVEST THEORY BROWN-M
        BAKANOV SP       DISC FARAD       60          130
    ----------------37-J FRANKL INST-------     223    43
        DROZ-VIN. P      COMPT REND       60    251  2297
    ----------------38-ANN MATH----------      39    65
        HOANG PT         COMPT REND       60    250  1195
EINSTEIN MA--------*42*TR AM SOC CIVIL-----     107   561
        KNISELY MH       ANGIOLOGY        60     11   535
```

Figure 2.1
Extract from the first SCI showing citations in 1960 (mostly) to some of Einstein's papers. Source: E. Garfield, *American Documentation*, July 1963, p. 196.

SCI volumes were primarily used to perform simple bibliographic research. Finally, one could also purchase a set of electronic data directly from ISI. Figure 2.1 shows the typical content of a page from the first edition of SCI. We see the citations (mostly in 1960) to some of Albert Einstein's papers published between 1905 and 1942. Today, the paper version of the index no longer exists, and the three databases (SCI, AHCI, and SSCI) are combined in the WoS, which covers approximately 12,000 journals in all disciplines. Like the ISI database, the WoS is accessible via university libraries (or any other institutions) subscribing to the services of Thomson Reuters, the company that bought ISI in 1993.

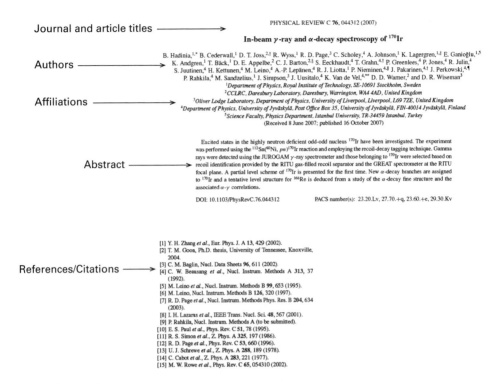

Journal and article titles ⟶

PHYSICAL REVIEW C **76**, 044312 (2007)

In-beam γ-ray and α-decay spectroscopy of ^{170}Ir

Authors ⟶

B. Hadinia,[1,*] B. Cederwall,[1] D. T. Joss,[2,†] R. Wyss,[1] R. D. Page,[3] C. Scholey,[4] A. Johnson,[1] K. Lagergren,[1,‡] E. Ganioğlu,[1,5] K. Andgren,[1] T. Bäck,[1] D. E. Appelbe,[2] C. J. Barton,[2,§] S. Eeckhaudt,[4] T. Grahn,[4,†] P. Greenlees,[4] P. Jones,[4] R. Julin,[4] S. Juutinen,[4] H. Kettunen,[4] M. Leino,[4] A.-P. Lepänen,[4] R. J. Liotta,[1] P. Nieminen,[4,‖] J. Pakarinen,[4,†] J. Perkowski,[4,¶] P. Rahkila,[4] M. Sandzelius,[1] J. Simpson,[3] J. Uusitalo,[4] K. Van de Vel,[4,**] D. D. Warner,[2] and D. R. Wiseman[3]

Affiliations ⟶

[1]*Department of Physics, Royal Institute of Technology, SE-10691 Stockholm, Sweden*
[2]*CCLRC, Daresbury Laboratory, Daresbury, Warrington, WA4 4AD, United Kingdom*
[3]*Oliver Lodge Laboratory, Department of Physics, University of Liverpool, Liverpool, L69 7ZE, United Kingdom*
[4]*Department of Physics, University of Jyväskylä, Post Office Box 35, University of Jyväskylä, FIN-40014 Jyväskylä, Finland*
[5]*Science Faculty, Physics Department, Istanbul University, TR-34459 Istanbul, Turkey*

(Received 8 June 2007; published 16 October 2007)

Abstract ⟶

Excited states in the highly neutron deficient odd-odd nucleus ^{170}Ir have been investigated. The experiment was performed using the ^{112}Sn(^{60}Ni, pn)^{170}Ir reaction and employing the recoil-decay tagging technique. Gamma rays were detected using the JUROGAM γ-ray spectrometer and those belonging to ^{170}Ir were selected based on recoil identification provided by the RITU gas-filled recoil separator and the GREAT spectrometer at the RITU focal plane. A partial level scheme of ^{170}Ir is presented for the first time. New α-decay branches are assigned to ^{170}Ir and a tentative level structure for ^{166}Re is deduced from a study of the α-decay fine structure and the associated α-γ correlations.

DOI: 10.1103/PhysRevC.76.044312   PACS number(s): 23.20.Lv, 27.70.+q, 23.60.+e, 29.30.Kv

References/Citations ⟶

[1] Y. H. Zhang *et al.*, Eur. Phys. J. A **13**, 429 (2002).
[2] T. M. Goon, Ph.D. thesis, University of Tennessee, Knoxville, 2004.
[3] C. M. Baglin, Nucl. Data Sheets **96**, 611 (2002).
[4] C. W. Beausang *et al.*, Nucl. Instrum. Methods A **313**, 37 (1992).
[5] M. Leino *et al.*, Nucl. Instrum. Methods B **99**, 653 (1995).
[6] M. Leino, Nucl. Instrum. Methods B **126**, 320 (1997).
[7] R. D. Page *et al.*, Nucl. Instrum. Methods Phys. Res. B **204**, 634 (2003).
[8] I. H. Lazarus *et al.*, IEEE Trans. Nucl. Sci. **48**, 567 (2001).
[9] P. Rahkila, Nucl. Instrum. Methods A (to be submitted).
[10] E. S. Paul *et al.*, Phys. Rev. C **51**, 78 (1995).
[11] R. S. Simon *et al.*, Z. Phys. A **325**, 197 (1986).
[12] R. D. Page *et al.*, Phys. Rev. C **53**, 660 (1996).
[13] U. J. Schrewe *et al.*, Z. Phys. A **288**, 189 (1978).
[14] C. Cabot *et al.*, Z. Phys. A **283**, 221 (1977).
[15] M. W. Rowe *et al.*, Phys. Rev. C **65**, 054310 (2002).

Figure 2.2
Typical information contained in a scientific article and registered in a citations index like the SCI.

Bibliometric databases do not contain the full text of articles, but rather a set of metadata associated with each paper. Typically recorded are the title of the article, the journal in which it was published, the names of all authors, their institutional affiliation, the type of document (article, letter, editorial, book review, etc.), and the complete list of references contained therein (figure 2.2). It is the list of references that gives the WoS (and now Scopus) its specificity compared to other kinds of bibliographic sources. And since these references sometimes include patents, this feature made possible the analysis patent citations.[1] Conversely, patent databases, which also contain references to scientific papers, would also be used, starting in the 1980s, to establish links between scientific research and technological innovation.[2]

Once computerized, all this information is reorganized to form a database. Queries combining different fields (authors, countries, institutions, journals, etc.) can thus be formulated to get results at different scales of analysis. What would have taken months of work using the paper copies of SCI in the 1970s can now be done in hours, if not minutes, a fact that contributes to the inflation of the number of papers using bibliometric data in all disciplines.

In its paper format, the SCI identified only the first author of a cited paper, even though most items were usually written by more than one researcher. This choice was made to simplify data acquisition and limit costs at a time when computers were big and slow. This pragmatic choice limited the possibilities of analysis, for it would have taken a lot of time to find, for example, citations to authors who, as the head of the laboratory, usually came last in the list. As early users of the SCI, sociologists of science thus suggested that databases include all the names (or at least that of the last author), for the reason just mentioned. Garfield, aware of the costs involved in such a change, responded by recalling that the SCI "was not created as a tool for measuring the performance of scientists! It was, and remains, primarily a tool for information retrieval. As such, the first author, year, journal, volume, and page [are] more than sufficient as an identifier."[3] With improvements in computer technology, and with the rising demand from research evaluation, bibliometric databases now include the complete list of cited authors, thus making their use possible (and also easier) for evaluation purposes.

A Tool for Historians and Sociologists of Science

From its origins, the SCI was seen as a potentially useful resource for historians and sociologists of science. Even before the publication in 1963 of the first version, Garfield had secured the support of the father of the sociology of science, Robert King Merton, as well as that of the historian of science and great promoter of bibliometrics, Derek de Solla Price. Garfield was himself very much interested in the history of science, and throughout his career, he worked on the development of computer programs that automatically deployed networks of citations among articles[4]. This interest in the history of science on the part of Garfield and his firm ISI culminated in the creation in 1981, thanks to a grant from the National Science Foundation (NSF), of a *Physics Citation Index* for the period 1920–1929. Supervised by Henry Small, who had been trained as a historian of science and was then director of research at ISI, this special index covered the period when quantum mechanics developed, and thus allowed researchers to study in detail a major scientific revolution from a bibliometric perspective for the first time.[5] This original interest in the utility for historians of a citation index ultimately led to the construction by Thomson Reuters of a retrospective database covering major scientific journals since 1900, both for the social sciences (the SSCI) and the natural sciences (the SCI).[6] The extensive use of citation data in the sociology of science during the 1970s also gave rise to close scrutiny of the limitations of that indicator—limitations that were restated by scientists in the 1990s when citations became part of the evaluation process.[7]

Over the years, research has established the aggregate properties of publications, references, and citations—properties that are essential to know in order to build valid indicators that can then be used to measure, at various scales, changes in the landscape of science. First, it is important to observe that the number of citations obtained by a typical paper depends on the number of references contained in the citing articles, and this propensity to cite varies widely between disciplines. It is obvious that the higher the number of references, the higher the chances of being cited, all other things being equal. Likewise, for a given propensity to cite, the number of citations will depend on the size of the community, keeping constant the number of papers per person. Even such a simplified model is sufficient to reproduce the pattern of citation observed over the twentieth century.[8] Today, the data show that the number of references per article has increased significantly over time, reflecting the exponential growth in the number of researchers and published articles and the pressure to cite related papers (figure 2.3a). Since the productivity of researchers has not grown significantly[9], the average number of citations per article has accordingly increased over time (figure 2.3b). It follows that the absolute number of citations means little in itself or in comparison with other disciplines and always should be interpreted in relation to the practices of the discipline of the researcher at a given time. Not surprisingly, biomedical sciences have the most cited articles, and humanities the least cited, not because of their different "scientific impact," but mainly as a consequence of the different citing cultures of these fields.

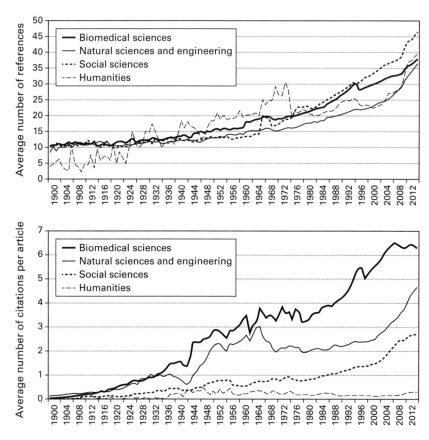

Figure 2.3
(a) Growth of the average number of references contained in articles by disciplinary fields, 1900–2014 (source: WoS); (b) growth of the average number of citations per paper (two years after publication) for major scientific fields, 1900–2012 (source: WoS).

It was also quickly established that the proportion of authors' self-citations in articles is generally low (around 8%) and understandably higher for journals' self-citations—that is, citations to articles from the same journal (around 20%). In all cases, the distribution of citations is highly skewed and is similar to that of the production of papers.[10] As shown in figure 2.4, the distribution of publications, citations, and research grants follow, for a large number of researchers, what is known as *Pareto distributions,* power laws of the form aX^{-y}, of which Lotka's law (already mentioned in chapter 1) is a particular case of such very skewed distributions with $y = 2$.[11] These

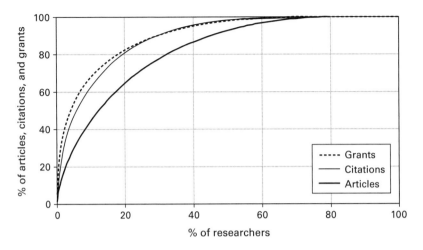

Figure 2.4
Distribution of grants, publications, and citations for a group of Quebec researchers (source: Observatoire des sciences et des technologies, OST).

distributions do not stray too far from the 20/80 rule of thumb: about 20% of researchers are usually responsible for roughly 80% of citations as well as grants. Publications are somewhat less concentrated, with 20% of research-ers producing only 60% of the articles. The higher concentration of cita-tions and grants makes sense when one notes that they depend more than publications on mechanisms of scientific recognition, which are affected by the sociological phenomenon of the "Matthew effect," which tends to attri-bute more credit to those who already have some, thus tending to accentu-ate inequalities.[12]

By the mid-1960s, researchers looked for correlations between the num-ber of citations and various social variables characterizing the researchers in order to identify the determinants of scientific productivity and impact. Thus, a study published in 1966 established that there was no correla-tion between the researchers' IQ and the level of their citations. However, research did show that the citation level was correlated with the prestige of the university that awarded the doctorate, the prestige scale being defined using expert panels.[13] Using the Science Citation index covering the year 1961, Garfield established that the 1962 and 1963 Nobel Prize winners were cited thirty times more than the average of all researchers.[14] Further work

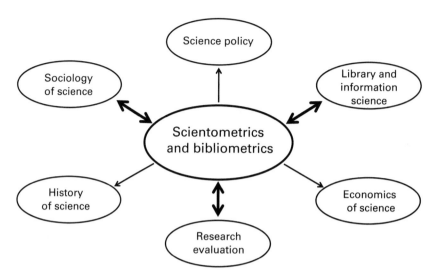

Figure 2.5
Major domains of application of bibliometrics.

later confirmed the link between citations, productivity, and the degree of recognition of researchers at the aggregate level.[15]

In short, because they cover a long period of time and survey, although unevenly, all knowledge fields, the WoS bibliometric databases (and, more recently, Scopus) provide a unique tool to study the social and conceptual changes of science in several disciplines and throughout the twentieth century at the global level. As shown in figure 2.5, one can use bibliometric data to analyze the development of science from an historical, sociological, economic, or political angle and at different scales from the micro (individual) to the macro (country or world) level.

Counting at Different Scales

At its most basic level, doing bibliometrics consists of counting documents. This counting can be done at different scales depending on the type of information contained in the documents or included in the database. Many scientific journals used only initials and last names in bylines, so counting individual papers involves the difficult problem of homonyms.[16] Worse, the cited documents often indicate only the name of the first author, thus making it even more difficult to count the citations to an author who is rarely first in the list of his or her multiple-author papers. Fortunately, most journals include the name of the home institution and the country, making it easier to analyze scientific output and impact at larger scales like the institution (hospital, laboratory, university, industry) and the country. Although university departments are not always indicated, the discipline, or even specialty, of the paper can be inferred from the domain covered by specialized journals (mathematics or genetics, for instance), but not for general scientific journals like *Science* or *Nature* that cover many different domains. Keywords from the titles or abstract can also be used to define the content of the paper. These very simple counting operations can provide a first good picture of the relative development of various fields of research in different institutions and countries, and in turn help us to understand various aspects of the structure and dynamics of science.

As we saw in the previous chapter, long before the advent of the SCI in the early 1960s, several scientists had begun the analysis of the evolution of the number of publications in their disciplines. In 1935, studying the growth curve of publications in the field of nitrogen fixation by plants, agricultural researchers even proposed a simple mathematical model— since then regularly rediscovered—that generated a logistic curve characterized by an exponential growth followed by saturation.[17] At the institutional level, researchers from the General Electric Research Laboratory in New York have shown that the analysis of publications is a useful method to identify the most active laboratories involved in a given research area or to evaluate the level of fundamental research going on in industrial laboratories.[18]

Although these early works were labor intensive and could cover only a limited field, they confirmed the value of such quantitative analyses of science. Now, computer-based bibliometric research can swiftly analyze all scientific disciplines and cover most countries, though often unevenly[19]. Taking into account the biases inherent in different databases, analysis of scientific production over time, on the scale of a country, region, or institution, provides important information about the growth or decline in certain research areas that is otherwise impossible to obtain. In fact, no scientist, however expert in his or her own field, can have access to the global structure of research without bibliometric data, which provide essential indicators to track the changing research trends and the emergence of new fields. As shown in figure 2.6, the meteoric rise of Chinese scientific production in the second half of the 1990s is evident among Brazil, Russia, India, and

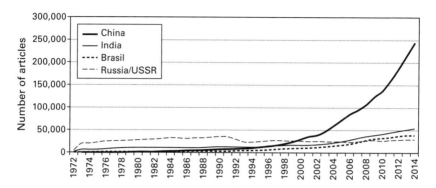

Figure 2.6
Evolution of the number of publications in BRIC countries, 1972–2014 (source: WoS).

China (the BRIC countries). This simple bibliometric data also confirms the rapid fall of the scientific output of Russia after the breakup of the Soviet Union in the early 1990s, as well as its rise in the 2000s.[20] One could produce similar figures for subfields (like physics, chemistry, and medical or engineering specialties) and define a specialty index to measure the relative presence of a country in a given field.[21] Once such national series of data are established, they can be correlated with global economic variables like gross domestic product (GDP). As might be expected, the total number of publications of a given country (as well as the number of patents, for that matter[22]) are strongly linked to its GDP, a sign that scientific development is closely associated with economic development.[23]

Disciplinary Differences

By leveraging information contained in scientific publications, bibliometrics can track the transformation of research practices over the twentieth century and the differences between disciplines. Hence, academics commonly divide the research world into the science, technology, engineering, and mathematics (STEM) and social sciences and humanities (SSH) fields. But a bibliometric analysis of the properties of the references contained in scientific articles shows that we deal with four distinct worlds instead of two. Biomedical research, for example, behaves a little differently from the rest of the natural sciences and engineering. And, although usually classified in the same group, SSH areas have specific citation practices, issuing from different traditions. Hence, almost three-quarters of the references contained in articles pertaining to the humanities refer to books, not journal articles. This proportion is relatively stable over time. By contrast, in economics, the proportion of references to books has steadily declined, from 55% to 30%, over the last forty years. This trend is understandable, as economists tend to mimic the behavior of the natural sciences, where more than 80% of the references are to journal articles; they thus cite books less often as if they were less scientific than papers. Interestingly, the social sciences lie between the humanities and the natural sciences and refer as often to books as to academic papers.[24]

Although often only descriptive, bibliometric data are important because they clearly demonstrate that publication practices vary widely by discipline. Therefore, it is dangerous to impose a single publication model based on the production of articles in specialized journals. Books, as well as individual book chapters, are still important in SSH, but as we will see in chapter 3, they tend to lose their value in the eyes of evaluators who use simplistic indicators like the "impact factor," which are defined only for journals and cannot be used for books. Evaluation indicators should be adapted to the practices of the discipline, not vice versa.

Publication practices tend to change in order to perversely adapt to the indicators used in evaluation. Hence, social scientists and humanists are pushed to publish more journal articles instead of books or book chapters, as the latter take more time to be cited and cannot be attributed an impact factor. Interestingly, the choice to write books or articles is, in the social sciences, also influenced by sociological variables such as places of training and hiring. In American universities, for instance, sociologists in private universities focus on publishing books, while their counterparts at public universities prefer to write journal articles.[25] Knowing the differences between the publication practices in the SSH area, as illustrated through citation analysis, can be very useful for identifying unsuitable evaluation criteria imposed upon the practitioners of these disciplines based on a misunderstanding of the properties of citation-based indicators.

Collectivization and Internationalization of Research

The evolution of the average number of authors per article (figure 2.7) and the proportion of articles with more than one author (figure 2.8) provides

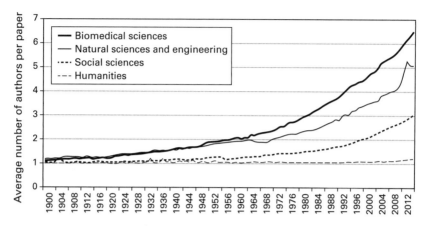

Figure 2.7
Average number of authors per paper in the major disciplinary fields, 1900–2014 (source: WoS).

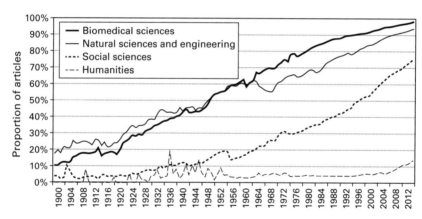

Figure 2.8
Proportion of papers with more than one author in the major disciplinary fields, 1900–2014 (source: WoS).

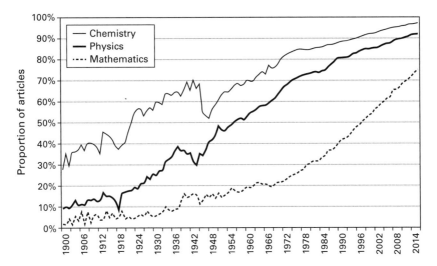

Figure 2.9
Proportion of papers with more than one author in chemistry, mathematics and physics, 1900–2014 (source: WoS).

another simple but revealing indicator of the collectivization of scientific research throughout the twentieth century. Within the natural sciences, for example, chemistry quickly became a team-based discipline, while mathematics remained grounded in individual work, much like the humanities. But despite the myth that mathematics is still an individualistic discipline, it has not been spared by the rise of collective research. As figure 2.9 shows, more than 50% of mathematics articles are now written by at last two authors. Individual disciplines can be decomposed into specialties that have distinct collaboration practices. Experimenters generally have larger teams than theorists, for example. That being said, the general trend is one of increased collectivization of research, and even the humanities, where the standard was predominantly one author per paper, responded to the pressure of collectivization over the last ten years and now has more than 13% of its papers with at least two authors.

Science has always been international in aim and scope, but bibliometric data allows us to follow the trend in a more precise manner. Since the late 1970s, the WoS database systematically includes the full address of all the authors. One can thus measure the evolution of international collaboration by measuring the proportion of papers involving multiple countries.

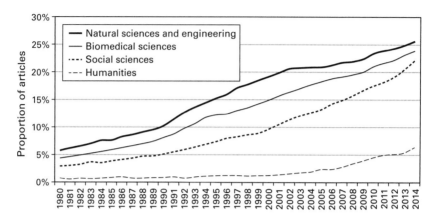

Figure 2.10
Proportion of papers written in international collaboration in the major disciplinary
fields, 1980–2014 (source: WoS).

Figure 2.10 shows the growth of international collaborations in the four
major disciplinary fields since 1980. The proportion of papers written in
international collaboration has increased steadily, with a visible acceleration in the early 1990s for the natural and biomedical sciences. Social
scientists have also seen an increase in their international collaboration
practices, and even an acceleration starting in 2000, with the humanities
following suit one decade later.

The more recent growth of international collaboration in the humanities, as measured by bibliometrics, can be explained first and foremost by
the fact that in these disciplines (i.e., history, philosophy, and literature),
the vast majority of papers had only one author until the beginning of
the twenty-first century (figure 2.8). Obviously, in this case, the indicator loses its validity as a measure of "internationalization" since it is based
on the premise that at least two addresses in different countries should be
present in the paper to count as an international collaboration. This obvious fact is a reminder that ignoring the manner in which an indicator has
been constructed could lead to erroneous conclusions, like saying that the
humanities are not international since the proportion of internationally
co-authored papers is low. In these fields, internationalization should be
measured using other indicators, like participation in international conferences and visits to or from foreign scholars.

In the natural sciences, by contrast, most papers have more than one author, so this publication-based indicator serves as a good measure of the process of internationalization of scientific research. These results clearly show that growth started well before the recent rhetoric on the internationalization and globalization of research, and that the trend grew first in response to the internal dynamics of science, although globalization was also stimulated recently by specific programs aimed at increasing international exchanges and collaborations.[26] The danger here, again, would be to apply to humanities the same measure as the one used for the natural sciences as if science were a universal, natural concept—which it is clearly not.

Scientific Networks

Far from being limited to the simple counting of publications, bibliometrics can build on more sophisticated tools, like network analysis, to represent patterns of scientific collaboration and relations between disciplines. One can thus literally map relations among countries or institutions; at the cognitive level, one can also map the relations among research domains. These measures take advantage of the fact that articles contain the addresses of all authors, thus defining a link between countries when at least two authors work in different countries. As an example, figure 2.11 shows the network of international collaborations between the fifty leading countries producing science between 2000 and 2005. It clearly shows the very strong scientific relations between the most productive countries (the United States, Japan, Germany, the United Kingdom, and France in decreasing order), which are surrounded by more peripheral countries whose collaboration network is often less diversified. Combining countries and disciplines, one can analyze differences in pattern of collaborations between countries according to disciplines: for instance, such relations can be high in physics and low in genetics, thus defining strategic relations between countries. On a lower scale, one could also map links between different institutions in the same country to obtain a representation of interinstitutional collaborations.

Constructing such networks for successive time periods, we can see that they are becoming denser. Not only is the proportion of publications written in international collaboration increasing, but the number of countries with which a given country works also has increased significantly since the 1980s, thus creating a denser web of international scientific collaborations.

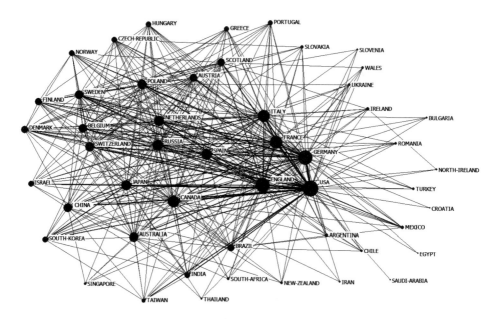

Figure 2.11

Network of international scientific collaborations between the fifty most productive countries (2000–2005). The diameter of the dot is proportional to the number of papers published by the country, and links are shown only if there are more than 500 collaborations between countries.

Discourse touting the importance of "interdisciplinarity" has been unrelenting over the last two decades. Bibliometrics can shed light on the dynamic relations between disciplines and measure their relative openness to outside influences. Although disciplinary boundaries are never impermeable, scientists tend to refer first to their own discipline. A simple way to measure such interchange between fields is to look at the intercitation network between citing and cited journals.[27] For any given network, one can calculate the centrality of the different nodes and thus provide a useful operational definition of the notions of *center* and *periphery*, which are often used as vague metaphors. By measuring changes in the centrality of a country or a journal over time, one can follow its path across the global scientific field. Applied to physics over the period 1900–1945, for example, this approach shows that whereas the German physics journal *Annalen der Physik*, which contains all the most famous papers by Albert Einstein, was indeed central in the discipline over the period 1900–1925, it was replaced by the American journal *Physical Review* over the next twenty years.[28] Dynamic bibliometric monitoring of science also shines a light on the emergence of new fields of research, such as nanotechnology and biotechnology. Using keywords contained in the articles (taken from the full text, the abstract, or the title) researchers and firms specializing in scientific and technological intelligence can thus be aware of recent research and discoveries in their fields of interest.[29]

Finally, citation analysis can be used to illuminate the conceptual links between articles. If two articles share a large proportion of their references, then it is likely that they deal with the same topic. It is this intuition that lies behind the method called *bibliographic coupling,* developed by Michael Kessler in the early 1960s to find related documents automatically.[30] A decade later, Henry Small devised a method called *co-citation analysis*, which links two documents that are often cited together in scientific papers.[31] As shown in figure 2.12, the two approaches are complementary and allow the construction of conceptual networks showing the connections (or lack thereof) between fields and subfields, making visible relatively distinct subsets. One can then use community detection techniques to automatically identify relatively autonomous disciplines in the entire field of science and distinct specialties within disciplines.[32]

Over the past ten years, much work has been devoted to the display of relations between disciplines.[33] Most of these representations show that the hierarchy of the sciences is not linear, as had been suggested by philosophers from Francis Bacon to Auguste Comte, but rather circular, as the Swiss psychologist and epistemologist Jean Piaget was one of the first to suggest.[34] Indeed, as shown in figure 2.13, it is mathematics that closes the loop, as the mathematical sciences connect the physical sciences on the one side to psychology and the social sciences on the other.[35]

All these examples, of which there are many more, suffice to show that bibliometric analysis can be put to good and sophisticated use to understand aspects of the historical and sociological dynamics of science, which would otherwise be difficult to access. These kinds of analyses go far beyond anecdotes, disciplinary bias, and arguments from authority, which are still too often used but cannot constitute a serious basis for decision making in science and technology policy. As recently pointed out in a report from the Council of Canadian Academies, bibliometric data can serve to inform and enlighten choices, but they cannot replace human decision-making

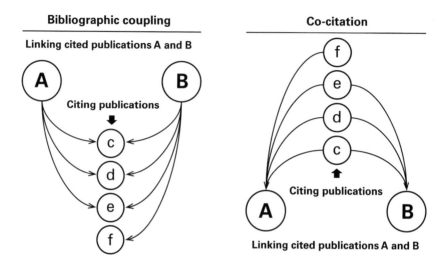

Figure 2.12

Bibliometric methods linking conceptually related documents: Bibliographic coupling relates documents A and B using their common references (c, d, and e); co-citation relates documents A and B, which are both cited in citing documents (c, d, and e). (Figure adapted from Eugene Garfield, "From Bibliographic Coupling to Co-Citation Analysis via Algorithmic Historio-Bibliography: A Citationist's Tribute to Belver C. Griffith," Lazerow Lecture presented at Drexel University, Philadelphia, November 27, 2001, 3, accessed December 21, 2015, http://garfield.library.upenn.edu/papers/drexelbelvergriffith92001.pdf.)

processes. Whatever the numbers may be for a given indicator, they cannot lead to any individual policy decision by themselves.[36]

A Few Myths on Citation Practices

Many myths and clichés about citation practices that circulate among scientists do not survive a serious bibliometric analysis of the data. It is, for example, very common to hear that only papers that are less than four or five years old are read and cited, and that the rapid growth in the number of publications increases the tendency to refer only to the most recent results. But a comprehensive study of the temporal evolution of the average (or median) age of references contained in scientific papers shows that the average and median age have actually increased over the last thirty years.[37] Similarly, the idea that most articles are never cited is false: the proportion

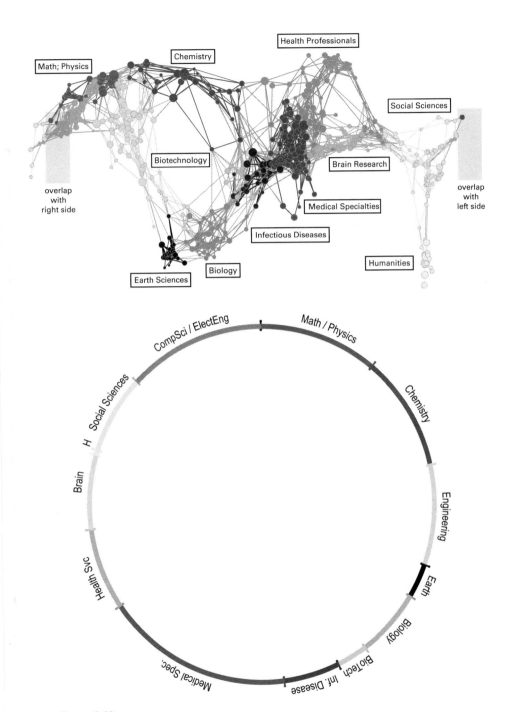

Figure 2.13
A map of the relations between the main sciences that shows the circular links connecting social sciences on the right with mathematics on the left (source: Börner, Katy, Richard Klavans, Michael Patek, Angela Zoss, Joseph R. Biberstine, Robert Light, Vincent Larivière, and Kevin W. Boyack. [2012]. Design and update of a classification system: The UCSD map of science. *PLoS ONE* 7, no. 7 [2012]: e39464).

of noncited articles actually has been decreasing over time, especially since the 1970s.[38] Measuring the proportion of uncited articles obviously depends on the time frame used for citing a given item. If it is limited to a two-year window, as is usually the case, it is clear that the proportion of noncited items will be larger in the social sciences than in the natural and biomedical sciences, for reasons related to the time it takes to publish articles in these different fields. However, if one increases this observation window to five or ten years, for example, the proportion of uncited items in social sciences decreases and becomes comparable to that of the natural sciences.[39] These data remind us that the temporality of scientific research greatly varies between disciplines.

Those who oppose citation analysis often invoke the so-called fact that erroneous or even fraudulent results may be highly cited and that, conversely, truly innovative work may stay uncited for a while. However, from the standpoint of the history and sociology of science, this is not a problem. On the contrary, the study of these citations illuminates the dynamics of scientific controversies and knowledge dissemination. It allows us to characterize the reception of a theory without having to judge whether it is good or not; indeed, this question can be decided only by the scientific community itself. Take the case of cold fusion, announced with great fanfare in 1989 by the electrochemists Stanley Pons and Martin Fleischmann. A bibliometric study published in the following year showed that just ten months after the announcement of their "revolutionary discovery" that nuclear fusion was possible at room temperature in a test tube, 52% of the citations were negative, 27% positive, and the rest were neutral. Interestingly, the positive citations came from theorists who attempted to explain the phenomenon.[40] As for the negatives, its proportion is much higher than the 15% suggested by a sample of thirty papers published in *Physical Review* between 1968 and 1972.[41]

The absence of citations to a given article does not necessarily show its low quality, but simply that scientists are not yet interested in the topic being treated. Scientists can discover an interest in such a topic much later and begin to cite an old article. In bibliometrics, this phenomenon is known as "Sleeping Beauty."[42] For example, a physics paper by the Italian physicist Ettore Majorana on the relativistic theory of particles with arbitrary spin, published in 1937, "slept" until the mid-1960s, when a number of new particles with different spin were found in accelerators, thus giving

Majorana's theory a timeliness it did not have in the 1930s, when only protons and electrons of one-half spin were known. Note, however, that Majorana was not unknown at the time, as his other important contributions were highly cited.[43]

Another cliché that circulates among scientists affirms that major discoveries like those of Einstein or the structure of the DNA waited many years to be cited. Thus, in a paper often cited by critics of biliometrics, the British biologist Peter Lawrence wrote that the most important article of the twentieth century was rarely mentioned during the first ten years following its publication.[44] As the article in question was that of James Watson and Francis Crick on the structure of DNA, published in *Nature* in 1953, I found this claim intriguing since the two researchers won the Nobel Prize in 1963, only ten years after their discovery, a time that seemed short compared to the usually much longer time lag between discovery and prize.[45] In this context, it seemed unlikely that the paper was ignored. So I started a detailed analysis of the citations to this article between 1953 and 1970, and I concluded that Lawrence's statement was a myth due to a misuse of bibliometrics, based on interpreting the absolute number of citations without taking into account the context and the type of journals citing that foundational paper. When done with the rigor needed, including appropriate calibrations, we find that, far from being ignored, Watson and Crick's paper actually was the most cited of all papers published in *Nature* in 1953, and remained so until 1970. Between 1953 and 1955, for example, it was cited thirty-six times more than the average number of citations received by all *Nature* papers published in 1953, and between 1956 and 1958, this proportion rose to sixty-five times more than the average. If one notes that the average number of citations to *Nature* papers is already much higher than that of all the journals of biology, it is clear the Watson and Crick paper was highly visible from the very beginning. In short, the sociological intuition was correct: such basic items do not really go unnoticed within the relevant scientific community, and this fact is adequately reflected in the citation data.[46]

As these examples show—and others might be added[47]—it is possible to study from historical and sociological points of view the publications and citations of a single researcher or a single paper without falling into the traps of evaluation and rankings.[48]

Effect of the SCI on Citation Practices

Following the publication of the first volumes of the SCI, it became clear to many observers that this new tool would affect how scientists and journal editors perceive the practice of citing. For example, Garfield encouraged journal editors and reviewers to make sure that authors cited all the relevant literature properly. He firmly believed that such proper citations would diminish the risk of losing time and money in redoing a given piece of research.[49]

According to Norman Kaplan, who in the mid-1960s was the first sociologist to write about the question of citation practices, this self-awareness contributes to making citation standards more explicit.[50] For many centuries, citation was in fact implicit and unsystematic, thus giving rise to priority disputes. In the first scholarly journals that were published in the mid-seventeenth century, citations to prior work often consisted of a vague reference to a person named in the body of the text. This practice responded to the implicit norm of the scientific community that urged authors to recognize previous contributions by community members and thus to acknowledge the priority of discovery. From the functional point of view of the scientific community, citation thus constitutes a credit allocation mechanism.[51]

Citations also allow an author to make explicit his or her position in a research tradition. For a long time, its use was informal and little codified. According to de Solla Price, systematization in the use of references is perceptible from the mid-nineteenth century.[52] However, Charles Bazerman observed that even in the late nineteenth century, more than half of the references in the journal *Physical Review* were still undated.[53] But the fact that the format was not well codified did not prevent referees and editors from asking authors to add references when needed to assure proper recognition of previous work. Thus, in the 1760s and 1770s, the publications committee of the Paris Academy of Sciences often required authors to cite previous work on a given subject. For example, a corresponding member of the Academy, Pierre-Toussaint Navier, who submitted a paper on the dissolution of mercury in acid, was asked by the members of the committee to "add the citations mentioned in the referee's report." Similarly, in 1765, the committee required the well-known savant, the Abbé Nollet, "to cite what was said" before him on his chosen topic of the behavior of small fish.[54]

The dissemination of the use of the SCI in scientific communities thus changed citation practices by making the act of citing more and more self-conscious on the part of authors, as well as better monitored by journal editors and reviewers. Along the way, all the details of references came to be formatted with clear indication of journal names, year of publication, complete first name (instead of initials), etc. The rise of bibliometric evaluations in the 1990s clearly stimulated the companies that sell these products (Thomson Reuters and Elsevier) to include more and more relevant information into their databases in order to make them more valuable for that new market niche. Whereas only a few pieces of data (i.e., name, journal, year) suffice to retrieve a paper, much more is needed to use citations for evaluation purposes.

The new importance given to citations as a measure of the quality or impact of research gave rise in the mid-1970s to many studies devoted to better understanding of the determinants of citation practices.[55] Most scientometricians agree that muliple motivations govern the choice of citations and that citing serves several functions. Citations can refer to facts, theories, methods, and sources of data. One thus cites books, patents, articles, and other sources. Since the mid-1970s, many classifications have been proposed to characterize different types of citations (affirmative, negative, neutral, perfunctory) and the motivations that an author may have to refer to an article or not.[56] Notwithstanding the variety of personal reasons to cite papers, it is essentially the aggregate properties of citations that count. From this point of view, the various reasons to cite cancel each other out, giving rise to an aggregate function. In other words, whatever the specific reasons that one may have to cite a given author or to choose not to, that does not really affect the general trends. For instance, Einstein was highly cited in the physics community in the 1920s, even though some would not cite him for ideological or racial reasons.[57]

Beyond the diversity of practices, the citation remains, at the most general level, a measure of the scientific visibility of a work, a global visibility that hides multiple uses, including rhetorical ones (that is to say, their persuasive function).[58] The fact that researchers often cite "classic" articles only to show how their work is part of a legitimate tradition that gives weight to their own work, even when they did not really use the cited papers, only confirms that the cited articles are indeed important in the eyes of the scientific community.

One of the perverse effects that one can imagine of the rising conscious-
ness of the importance of citations is the supposed growth of self-citations.
While it is relatively easy to remove them to assess the real visibility of a
researcher, the proportion of self-citations, contrary to what many seem to
think,[59] has remained fairly stable since 1980.[60] In short, the practice of self-
citation is not really a problem, especially as it has a legitimate function:
namely, to recall previous work upon which the current research is built.
In fact, the motivations for self-citations are similar to the ones invoked for
citing other authors.[61]

The many criticisms of citation analysis—some justified, some less so,
as has been discussed—have gained momentum in many scientific communities over the last twenty years as a reaction against the proliferation of
research evaluations at both the individual and institutional level. Indeed,
criticizing self-citations or citation of "buddies" makes sense when, for evaluation purposes, papers and citations are transformed from units of knowledge and recognition into simple accounting units that can be monetized.
It is, therefore, time to address the issue of research assessment based on
bibliometrics.

3 The Proliferation of Research Evaluation

The current discussion concerning the importance of research evaluation can easily lead to the impression that researchers have existed for a long time without ever being evaluated. It is thus necessary to undo this misconception by recognizing that the assessment of research dates back to the very beginning of the institutionalization of science in the mid-seventeenth century. It then spread to other levels of organization with the emergence of new structures related to the organization of research, such as laboratories, departments, and universities. In short, for more than 350 years, researchers have never ceased to be evaluated, and people in this type of occupation are probably the most constant targets of assessment.

The problem is thus less that of evaluation itself than its proliferation and frequency, which has had the effect of increasing the number of demands made on researchers to evaluate their colleagues, to the point that many now refuse these additional duties to preserve their time for research.[1] Although some researchers seem to think that intellectual work is impossible to evaluate, it may be useful to recall that evaluations through peer review already exist at various levels in the following areas:

• Publications and scholarly communications
• Research grant applications
• Teaching
• Promotions
• Departments and research centers
• Graduate programs
• Universities

Let us briefly recall how some of these assessments work.

The Evaluation of Scientific Publications

The beginning of research evaluation can be traced to the creation, in March 1665, of the *Philosophical Transactions of the Royal Society of London*. Edited by one of the two secretaries of this learned society, Henry Oldenburg, this journal is the prototype of the modern scholarly journal. Its content is limited to scientific research and includes original articles and republications of papers by foreign scientists, as well as book reviews and summaries. From the very inception of the project, its content was "reviewed by members of the Society."[2] Isaac Newton himself suffered at the hands of reviewers in 1672, when he submitted his first article on the spectrum of white light to the *Philosophical Transactions* journal. Appointed the rapporteur in this case, Robert Hooke found Newton's paper not very original, and even considered its conclusions erroneous in view of his own theory of light published seven years earlier—a theory that Newton had had the temerity to ignore. This assessment was badly received by Newton, of course, and he decided never to submit another paper to that journal.[3]

For a long time, research evaluation was limited to the peer review of the scientific publications by colleagues and competitors in the scientific field. Journals, first general and then covering all scientific domains, became more specialized during the nineteenth century, dedicated to a specific discipline (such as chemistry, mathematics, or physics) or even a specialty (such as optics or virology), catering to a specific group of practitioners of the same subject.[4]

Until the early twentieth century, the peer review system remained quite informal, the editor and the editorial committee deciding whether they had the expertise to assess the submitted paper or to send it to a colleague for further evaluation. The rejection rate was generally very low. The German physicist Max Planck estimated that fewer than 10% of the papers submitted to the *Annalen der Physik*, the flagship journal of physics at the turn of the twentieth century, were rejected. As editor, he much preferred to ask for corrections than to announce to a colleague his refusal to publish.[5]

As a sign of the slow evolution of this informal system, in 1936, Albert Einstein, probably used to seeing his papers immediately accepted, was surprised and annoyed to learn that the article that he had proposed to the American journal *Physical Review* had been sent to a reviewer who had prepared an anonymous report, in which he stated that the great scientist had made a mistake in his calculations. Upon receiving that negative report, Einstein responded that he never authorized the editor to show his paper to anyone before publication and saw no reason to respond on what he considered erroneous comments by an anonymous author. He concluded his letter to the editor of the journal by saying that he simply withdrew his paper. He obviously ignored the mode of operation of that scientific journal, which was more formal than that of most European journals in which he had published before moving to the United States. The irony is that Einstein did take the comments into account after all, and he published the following year a modified version of his article in another journal.[6] This may serve as a reminder that, thanks to the serious peer review process of scientific publications, even great minds can be saved from losing face by publishing flawed results that would have had to be retracted or corrected.

The Evaluation of Research Projects and Laboratories

In the course of the twentieth century, government funding for research has become institutionalized in most countries, and the same peer review process is used to sift through research grant applications and select those that merit funding. In 1901, for example, a scientific research fund was created in France to help individual researchers. In 1916, the National Research Council of Canada started to distribute grants-in-aid to university researchers who submitted scientific projects.[7] In the United States, the federal government created the National Science Foundation (NSF) in 1950 to provide money to American scientists who had heretofore depended mainly on private philanthropy instead of government assistance.[8] Similar organizations, in addition to private philanthropic foundations that also use peer review committees, now exist in most countries and usually cover all research domains. Their policy is to contribute to the advancement of knowledge on the basis of short-term research projects (usually lasting three to five years) instead of long-term allocations to research institutions.

In these granting agencies, evaluation usually takes the form of face-to-face exchanges in committees of between 10 and 20 members. These evaluations, also based on external referees' written reports, have long remained fairly informal and little standardized, the dynamics of exchanges around the table aiming to reach a consensus in the selection of the best projects. As shown by sociologists Jonathan and Stephen Cole, the system suffers from a large degree of randomness, with the same projects being evaluated very differently depending on the composition of the panel.[9] The criteria used by members of the evaluation committees are also known to vary greatly depending on the discipline, and if they are consistent in any way, it is in their vagueness: what is found "exciting" and "original" by one member may be considered "incoherent" and "methodologically weak" by another.[10]

In order to try to control the obvious subjectivity of the evaluations, more formal and quantitative systems have been gradually implemented that allow calculations based on the individual rating of board members, thus constructing a collective evaluation and ranking. However, despite appearances to the contrary, this so-called arithmetic does not change the fact that the decision to select "2.5" instead of "4.0" in the software remains an unanalyzed subjective choice. This pseudo-quantification of judgments, which forces the reviewer to put "3" instead of "Excellent!" or "1.5" instead of "Rubbish!" does not affect the fundamentally subjective nature of the judgment but merely hides it behind the apparent objectivity of a number.[11]

The most important effect of this transformation is to make the various results of the committee members commensurable: being numbers, they can now be combined in various ways to calculate the "average" of all judgments and identify the "variance" to focus the deliberations on those assessments that deviate significantly from this average, interpreted as the "consensus." If all members have checked off "2," then the consensus seems total, and the project is rejected, compared to the one whose average is 3.5. These numbers make the decision easy even if behind the same mark, each evaluator may, in fact, base his or her judgment on different subjective criteria. The model, therefore, remains based on collective deliberations to arrive at a consensual (or at least a majority) decision for choosing the best projects, and the numerical assessments serve as a way to control the exchanges and focus them to converge more quickly toward a collective decision.

The use of bibliometric methods in research evaluation emerged in the context of mounting critiques of this relatively informal peer review system. In the mid-1970s, the NSF used citation analysis to check if the peer review process really allowed the selection of the best researchers. Defining quality on the basis of the number of citations, one study showed that, in chemistry, over 80% of NSF grants went to researchers cited more than 60 times, on average, in the previous five years; and that in the four academic departments that receive the majority of grants, researchers were cited about 400 times over the same period. These results were used to counter critics who claimed that the assessment process was fundamentally flawed.[12] Since then, such bibliometric analyses applied to departments, research groups, or universities have become routine in journals like *Scientometrics* and *Research Evaluation*.[13]

Professors and researchers are usually members of departments, laboratories, or research units, levels of organization that also became objects of evaluation using bibliometric methods during the 1980s. Comparative analysis that uses publication and citation indicators for departments or laboratories working in a given field or on a given object makes possible an evaluation of their performance and productivity on the basis of aggregate data for all members of the unit chosen for analysis. The number of papers per researcher, as well as normalized measures of citations to take field specificity into account, provide useful information at a level of aggregation that make results more stable than they would be for individuals.[14] Whereas aggregate citation data are clearly useful indicators, using them for evaluating individual researchers is more problematic, as we will see later in this chapter.

Since the first decade of the new millennium, the spread of basic bibliometric techniques and database has led to the multiplication of auto-analysis in many disciplines, based on descriptive statistics of publications and citations. The results are published in various disciplinary journals (e.g., economics, sociology, political science, medicine, management) instead of the specialized bibliometrics, information science, and research evaluation journals, as was the case in the previous decades. This democratization of bibliometrics is largely responsible for the dubious quality of many papers that are not peer-reviewed by experts in the field, but only by peers of the discipline being evaluated. Hence, the large corpus of knowledge already accumulated is too often ignored by scientists who reinvent the wheel instead of following Eugene Garfield's advice and beginning their research with a bibliographic search on the topic that they want to study.[15]

Evaluation of Individual Researchers

Another level of assessment, of course, is that of the researchers themselves. Since the creation of the University of Berlin in 1810, the model of the research university has become dominant in most countries, and the professor has been transformed into a researcher training future researchers at the doctorate and postdoctorate levels. Hiring institutions ask the advice of external experts before employing new faculty members or granting them tenure or promotion. Peer review is also the basic mechanism used at this level, and these peers make comprehensive and qualitative judgments about the value and originality of the candidate's work. After tenure, evaluation is often less frequent, and its nature varies greatly depending on the country and the institution.[16] Things started to change again in the 1970s, when bibliometrics began to be used at the level of individual researchers.

The question of the use of bibliometric data to assess individuals was raised at the very birth of the Science Citation Index (SCI), and Garfield himself immediately responded to these concerns. Projecting a strong image, he recalled that it would be absurd to attribute the Nobel Prize annually to the most cited authors, and added that, solely on the basis of citations of his work, Trofim Lysenko (a Russian biologist promoting the then-discredited theory of heredity of acquired characteristics in the 1940s and 1950s) would be considered one of the greatest scientists of the 1950s.[17] According to Garfield, citations provide access to articles and those who cite them, thus helping to make a judgment. The sheer number of citations cannot replace such a judgment, which must take into account other variables because citations vary according to the nature of the article published. A paper describing a method or a procedure is generally cited much more frequently, and for a longer time period, than a typical contribution to the advancement of knowledge; and a review article, which summarizes the state of knowledge on a given subject, also tends to be cited more often than a paper reporting a particular discovery.

An ardent promoter of his new product, Garfield claimed that citation analysis could predict future Nobel Prize winners.[18] This was an obvious exaggeration because, although Thomson Reuters also makes these predictions yearly to promote its product, the Web of Science (WoS), they are not realistic. They do not take into account the fact that the Nobel committees must weigh the great diversity of specialized research within a given discipline, as one cannot compare discoveries in astrophysics with theories in elementary particle physics or solid-state physics on the simple basis of citations. Strategic reasons thus greatly contribute to the final selection of Nobel Prize winners. Moreover, there are always too many highly cited authors in comparison with the very small number of Nobel Prizes awarded each year.[19]

For Garfield, it was obvious that any tool can be diverted from its legitimate uses, and it is up to "the scientific community to prevent misuse of SCI paying the necessary attention to its judicious use."[20] His position was the same for the use of his journal impact factor (IF), created to serve as a tool to aid in the selection of journals by libraries, which, as we shall see next, has been transformed, without critical reflection, from a tool designed for journals to one used to evaluate researchers and their papers. Despite these early calls for vigilance, which found few adherents, bibliometrics slowly began to be used in the 1970s in the evaluation process of individual researchers.

As noted by the social psychologist Janet Bavelas, changes in the academic world after the 1960s made the former method of appointing colleagues based on personal networks (i.e., old boy networks) and on the sole authority of deans or department heads unacceptable.[21] The quest for an evaluation system considered more "democratic" and "objective" and less arbitrary coincided with the availability of the SCI. Moreover, rapid growth in the number of professors and researchers during this period (1965–1975) accentuated the difficulty of assessing too many applicants, who could not all be known personally. Add to this the fact that numbers have an appearance of objectivity, and the conditions for the development of the use of citations as a so-called objective indicator of quality are met.[22]

In May 1975, the journal *Science* published a long analysis of the rise of the use of citations in the assessment of the scientific productivity of individual researchers. To contest what she considered an unfair treatment, a professor of biochemistry argued, on the basis of the number of citations received by her publications, that she was much more cited than her male colleagues being promoted at the same time.[23] This example shows that the use of citations as a measure of "quality" or "impact" of research is not only a tool in the hands of science administrators, but also a weapon that researchers themselves can use when the results favor them. Over the last decade, with easier access to citation databases such as Google Scholar, it has become common for scientists to include in their curriculum vitae the number of citations received by their articles, as well as their "h-index" (discussed in the next section), even if the value of these indicators is highly questionable and may even distort evaluation and hiring processes, as we will now see.

The H-Index Outbreak

In the mid-2000s, when the scientific community began to concoct bibliometric indexes to make individual evaluations more objective, the American physicist Jorge E. Hirsch, at the University of California at San Diego, made his own proposal: the h-index. This index is defined as being equal to the number N of articles published by a researcher that obtained at least N citations each. Thus, an author who published 20 items, of which 10 have been cited at least 10 times each since their publication, has an h-index of 10. The improvised nature of this index is already evident in the title of the article: "An Index to Quantify an Individual's Scientific Research Output."[24] Although published in a journal usually considered prestigious, the *Proceedings of the National Academy of Sciences*, this index is neither a measure of quantity (output) nor quality or impact; rather, it is a composite of them. It combines arbitrarily the number of articles published with the number of citations they received.

This new index was supposed to counter the use in the evaluation of researchers of the sheer number of published papers, since that indicator of productivity does not take into account the quality of the papers. According to a popular cliché, it would be easy to publish a large number of low-quality papers, so the number of published articles should be corrected to take into account their quality. The h-index purportedly provides a solution with a synthetic measure using a single number combining production and quality. The problem is that it was quickly shown that the h-index is itself very strongly correlated to the total number of published articles, so it does not really provide a measure of quality, independent of productivity.[25] More important, it has none of the basic properties (discussed in chapter 4) that any good indicator should possess. Finally, it has been shown that the h-index is incoherent in the way that it ranks researchers whose number of citations increases proportionally. Moreover, its value never decreases, which is certainly a bizarre feature for any indicator. Although it is supposed to be a valid measure of quality at any given time, the h-index in fact behaves like a thermometer that, once it measured 20 degrees on a given day, could only measure 21 or more degrees on the following days, whatever the real temperature is. It can thus be safely concluded that, in the words of Waltman and van Eck, the h-index "cannot be considered an appropriate indicator of a scientist's overall scientific impact."[26]

This poorly constructed index is actually quite noxious when used as an aid to decision making because it can generate perverse effects. A simple example will suffice to demonstrate its basic flaw as an indicator. Compare two scenarios: A young researcher who has published only 3 articles over the last five years, which were cited 60 times each in the following three years; and a second researcher, the same age, who is more prolific and has produced 10 papers over the same period, cited 11 times each. Therefore, this second researcher has an h-index of 10, while the former's h-index is only 3. Since any valid measure of a concept (here, "quality") should rise in a monotonic manner, one should conclude that 10 is much better than 3. But it is obvious that common intuition of scientific impact or quality would conclude that the researcher with 3 papers cited 60 times is the better researcher (more visible, with more impact). To reach that conclusion, though, one must compare two distinct kinds of indicators and thus two distinct goods: number of papers (as a measure of productivity) and number of citations (as a measure of visibility of the papers). The average or median numbers of citations per paper, normalized to take into account the specificity of each research domain, provide such a well-defined and adequate quality indicator.[27] By contrast, using the h-index can lead to betting on the wrong horse.

Despite these demonstrated technical defects, the use of the h-index has become widespread in many scientific disciplines. It seems tailor-made to satisfy the narcissism of many researchers.[28] Its rapid spread was also facilitated by the fact that it is now a "black-box" included in many databases, thus providing to its users an h index without any reflection and effort. It is certainly surprising to see scientists, who are supposed to have some mathematical training, lose all critical sense in the face of such a simplistic figure. Their behavior confirms the adage that has all the appearances of a social law: Any number beats no number.

According to Hirsch, his index promotes "a more democratic assessment of people's research."[29] On the contrary, everything suggests that by ignoring the conditions of validity of an indicator, this supposed "democracy" will quickly turn into evaluative populism, where everyone will throw numbers at the heads of competitors to declare that they are not as good as they may think. Reacting to the increasing uncontrolled use of bibliometrics, a committee of the International Mathematical Union noted that, "If one consults with doctors when practicing medicine, surely one ought to consult with statisticians when practicing statistics."[30] But given that their report seems to rediscover the usual properties and limitations of bibliometric data, known for decades by experts in scientometrics, one might also suggest that scientists (including mathematicians) using bibliometrics should consult bibliometricians.

Misuse of the Journal IF

The biggest problem caused by the use of citation data in research evaluation is probably the misuse of an indicator developed to measure the so-called impact of scientific journals. The production of scientific journals has become a highly profitable and competitive market, and journals now use the IF as a promotional tool to convince authors to submit them their best papers and to sell subscriptions to libraries. Since the late 1990s, the impact factor is seen not only as an indicator of the quality of the journals, but also—and wrongly, as will be seen—as a measure of the quality of the articles that appear in them. Not surprisingly, as we will see later in this chapter, the growing attention given to the IF has generated the ugly practice of trying to influence the referencing practices of scientists to make a journal's IF go up. To understand how a simple indicator can generate such extreme behavior, we must first recall the invention of the IF.

Published annually since 1975 by Thomson Reuters in its *Journal Citation Report* and calculated from the data contained in the WoS, the IF of a journal for a given year is a simple arithmetic mean of the total number of citations obtained that year by all the articles published in that journal in the previous two years. The IF, therefore, characterizes journals, not articles.[31] For example, the IF of a journal for 2006 is calculated by dividing the number of citations that articles published in 2004 and 2005 received in 2006, by the number of articles published during the previous two years (i.e., 2004 and 2005).

The (admittedly arbitrary) choice of a short time window of two years to assess the impact is not without consequences. It implicitly pits the high IF of scientific journals against the very low IF of social sciences and humanities journals. But this opposition is largely an artifact of the selected measurement time window because the temporality of research in the social sciences and humanities is longer than that in the natural and biomedical sciences. As we saw in chapter 1, the half-life of papers varies greatly according to discipline (figures 1.1a and 1.1b). As a result, increasing the citation window to ten years makes the IF of journals in social sciences disciplines reach comparable values to those in the natural sciences. For example, the average two-year-citation rate for articles of the medical journal *The Lancet* in 1980 was 2.4, and that of the *American Sociological Review* was 1.8. Calculated over a period of ten years, though, the results are very different: the IF of the sociology journal (20.9) greatly exceeds that of the medical journal (14.0).[32] It is perfectly obvious that the IFs of journals in different fields are not comparable, and that these numerical values makes sense only when compared with those of journals in the same research domain.

Another important characteristic of the IF is that it includes self-citations; that is, citations of the journal to itself in the total number of citations received. Although this issue goes back to the construction of the indicator in the early 1970s, it only emerged as a problem in the 1990s, when the IF became an important instrument in the competition between journals and started to be used as a proxy for measuring the quality of individual papers. Its strategic importance then led journal editors and owners to coerce authors to cite more articles from their own journal as an implicit condition for accepting to publish their papers.[33] By definition, the rising number of self-citations of journals had the effect of increasing their IFs, even when citations from outside journals (a better measure of visibility) did not change or even decreased. This undue pressure on authors began in the second half of the 1990s and has been much debated since.[34]

The problem is partly technical, since it would suffice to redefine the IF to exclude journal self-citations and thus make it more difficult to manipulate the index, for it would then require the formation of a cartel of journals exchanging citations. As we will see next, surprising as it may seem, some journals appear to have taken that desperate step. Although it still provides the usual values of IF based on the initial definition (including self-citations), the *Journal Citation Report* has adapted its product to take these possible manipulations into account and now also publishes an IF obtained by excluding journal self-citations. In addition, they also show the proportion of journal self-citations, which provides a useful indicator of external visibility.

The fact that some journals' editors have pushed authors to augment the number of citations to the papers published in their journals should not cause one to demonize journal self-citations, which are actually a normal practice. In truth, it makes perfect sense that articles published in the same journal should be somehow connected by their research object or topic and thus cite each other. Journals often serve a limited, specialized community. Take the case of the mathematical theory of knots. The journals that address this specialized field of research are obviously not legion. In fact, there is only one—the *Journal of Knot Theory and Its Ramifications*. Those experts who work on knot theory seek to publish in it, although other more general journals also accept articles on this topic.

What is the effect on its IF of removing self-citations from this journal? It obviously reduces it. Consulting the *Journal Citation Report* for 2009, we see that the IF of the *Journal of Knot Theory* is 0.523, but this figure drops to 0.311 when one removes self-citations, which contribute 40% of the total. Does that really change anything? In fact, its IF should not have any importance for evaluation, for it is clear that those working in the very specialized field of knot theory know whether this journal is good or not. And if another mathematical journal that also publishes only a few papers on knot theory has an IF of 0.822, that does not mean it is of better quality, since—all other things being equal—the IF depends on the size of the research area. If there are only 100 people on topic X, it will invariably receive fewer citations per paper (given a constant number of references in the papers) than if there were ten times more researchers on the same topic. It is not surprising, therefore, that for some very specialized areas, the rate of journal self-citations is high.

Some journals, however, appear to have abnormal citation levels. Wary that the controversy over the handling of IF could affect the value of its product, Thomson Reuters intervened in the debate and created in 2007 a "blacklist" of journals that were appearing to manipulate their IFs. As a sanction, Thomson Reuters does not publish a journal's IF when it thinks it is being manipulated. Nine journals were thus penalized in 2007.[35] This monitoring also includes citation exchanges between journals. This practice is more difficult to identify, but Thomson Reuters has developed softwares that allows its detection. Thus, in the 2013 edition of *Journal Citation*

Report, 37 journals were put in a different class, including 14 for reasons of citation exchanges. The previous year, only three journals were in this category. The offending journals remain blacklisted for two years before undergoing reassessment. It should be noted that this represents fewer than 1% of the journals listed in the WoS.[36]

Much as the pressure to publish generates scientific frauds, the overemphasis on IFs pushes journal editors into deviant behavior.[37] In the summer of 2013, the editor of the Brazilian medical journal *Clinics* was dismissed for seeking to maximize the number of citations obtained by his journal by participating in a citations cartel. This deviant behavior was a predictable perverse effect of a government policy that assessed the quality of graduate programs in Brazil on the basis of the IFs of journals in which students published.

Critical of this simplistic evaluation system, the editors of Brazilian journals demanded that it be amended.[38] It may indeed be quite normal for a national journal to seek to maximize the visibility of the articles that it publishes and ask authors to cite relevant national articles instead of referring only to foreign works. The lesson here should be that these manipulations of IFs would not have any importance and would not even have been perceived as deviant had the IF not been transformed into an evaluation criterion of researchers.[39]

Regardless of how it is calculated, the IF remains a measure related to the journal, not to the articles it contains. The fundamental reason that makes it a flawed indicator of the value of individual articles is that the distribution of actual citations received by the articles published in a given journal follows a power law similar to that of Alfred Lotka for productivity, which means that most articles are in fact cited very little. Only a few are very highly cited, and they inflate the value of the IF. For this type of distribution, the average is not a good measure of central tendency, which is valid only for the so-called normal or bell-shaped distribution.

As already noted in chapter 2, power laws in bibliometrics can usefully be summarized by the expression "20/80," meaning that only 20% of the items receive 80% of the citations (see figure 2.4). The magazine *Nature*, for example, whose editors admit that the IF should not be used for the evaluation of individual papers, is not an exception to that skewed distribution, even though it has one of the highest IFs. In 2004, for example, 89% of all the citations to that journal were generated by just 25% of the articles it published.[40] We are not very far from the 20/80 rule that summarizes the high concentration of such distributions.

In short, an article in a journal with high IF may in fact never be cited. If one wants to measure the quality or visibility of a particular item, one must look at the citations actually received in the years following its publication. But that of course takes time, and those who prefer "quick and dirty" evaluation do not want to wait three to five years. So they use the IF of the journal in which the papers are published as a proxy of their quality and impact, even though such a measure is totally inappropriate. As we will see later, it is the same impatience to evaluate that lies at the basis of the so-called altmetrics movement.

Despite the fact that since the mid-1990s, experts in bibliometrics have regularly called attention to the absurdity of using the IF to evaluate individual researchers[41], this has not prevented its unwarranted use by decision makers, as well as by many supposedly rational scientists on evaluation committees. Government officials and research organizations in a number of countries, like Pakistan, China, South Korea, and Japan, have even established financial incentives based directly on the numerical value of a journal's IF! As reported in the journal *Nature* in 2006, the Pakistan Ministry of Science calculated the sum of IFs of articles published over a year to set a bonus of between $1,000 and $20,000. In China, the Beijing Institute of Biophysics of the Chinese Academy of Sciences established a similar system at the time: An IF between 3 and 5 earns $250 per point, and $875 per point if the IF goes above 10. In such a context, it should come as no surprise that some Chinese researchers have been suspected of manipulating the peer-review system in order to get published in select journals, leading journal editors to retract papers on the basis that they had been fraudulently peer-reviewed by their authors.[42]

In an editorial in the same issue of *Nature*, the magazine denounced such nonsense.[43] In 2013, the editor of *Science*, Bruce Alberts, repeated that "this impact factor mania makes no sense."[44] About the same time, more than 400 scientific organizations and 10,000 individuals signed the San Francisco Declaration on Research Assessment (DORA), a manifesto insisting that the IF should not be used as a surrogate measure of the quality of individual research articles or to hire, promote, fund, or otherwise assess individual scientists.[45]

Whatever one may think of the productivity bonuses offered to researchers, the real problem here is that the indicator used is flawed. It is indeed impossible that the IF of the best journals of mathematics will ever equal the best medical journal. But no reasonable person would conclude that medical papers are better than mathematics papers, and therefore grant medical authors a higher bonus, on the simplistic basis of the values of the IF of the journals in which they publish.

Finally, it is worth noting the phony precision of journal IFs, which are "measured" to three decimal places! In science, there are very few natural phenomena that we can pretend to know with such exactitude. For instance, who wants to know that the temperature is 20.233 degrees Celsius? The obvious question is: Why not limit IF to one digit: 1, 2, 3 ... 20, 21, ... etc.? The equally obvious answer is that the various rankings based on IF would lose most of their value. Economists are particularly fond of ranking their journals using IFs.[46]

Therefore, consider the list of economics journals in the WoS and their IF values in 2011. Ranking 256 journals using IFs to three decimal places, it is obvious that few will be *ex aequo* on the same ranks (only three journals have an IF of 1.000, two of 0.757, and three to 0.743), thus allowing the assignment of, say, ranks 22 and 24 as if they were distinct. Now, given that no one can seriously claim that these decimals have any real meaning, let us look at the rankings obtained if you keep the IF to a single digit. One then sees that only two journals stand out, with an IF of 9 (*Journal of Economic Literature*) and 6 (*Quarterly Journal of Economics*), followed by two with identical IFs of 4, and then twelve with an IF of 3 and thirty-one with an IF of 2. Finally, 118 have an IF of 1. In summary: one cannot really distinguish within these large groups, and the addition of more decimal places is merely a method to create arbitrarily distinct rankings. An economist might tell us that one more decimal point is useful, but that still leaves four journals tied at 2.7 (rows 11–14) and eighteen in the club of the *World Bank Economic Review,* with an IF of 1.1 (rows 70–83). Here, a false precision hides a fundamental inaccuracy.

Misuse of rankings and indicators with a patina of precision basically betrays ignorance of the properties of the indicators used. I don't need to comment in more detail here on the many perverse effects generated by the use of flawed indicators.[47] Only the opportunism of researchers who benefit from miscalculated bonuses, and of journal editors who take advantage of the use of their IFs for evaluative purposes, may lead them to believe (or pretend to believe, anyway) that such a system is rational, let alone just and equitable.

The emergence in 2014 of the Nature Index, which ranks countries and institutions on the basis of the papers they publish in what they define as "high-quality science journals," offers an interesting case of a ranking created to capture part of the publication market. Contrary to the other rankings on the evaluation market, which are not produced by journal publishers, this one is the property of the Nature Publishing Group, owned by Macmillan and now merged with Springer, one of the largest publisher of scientific journals.[48] Based on only sixty-eight journals, including seventeen (25%) from the *Nature* group itself, the ranking is said to offer "a perspective on high-quality research on the basis of published articles" and to "provide institutions with an easy means to identify and highlight some of their best scientific research."[49]

Now, it should be obvious that taking such a ranking at face value would mean that institutions should pressure their researchers to publish in these journals and not elsewhere. Based on publication counts and not on citations or IFs, this new ranking in fact defines high-quality scientific research in a tautological manner—that is, what is being published in its chosen sixty-eight journals. Notwithstanding that major disciplines like mathematics are not represented in the "sampling," this trick can work on those who, after a few years, will naively interpret the results as a black box defining what high-quality scientific research is, and adapt their behavior to improve their position in this ranking. That development will be essentially profitable to the group that produces the index and the associated journals.

However, as is the case for the IF, the basic flaw of the Nature Index is that it takes a specific journal as a measure of the quality of a paper within it, instead of looking at the paper itself and the real citations it gets (or not). Given Lotka's distribution, publishing a paper in one of those sixty-eight journals is *not* proof that the scientific community will find it useful or interesting.

University Rankings

The ideology of rationalization, efficiency, and excellence, promoted since the 1980s by the so-called New Public Management, focused on the evaluation of everything using indicators and benchmarks as "objective" measures of efficiency and return on investment. In higher education and research, this ideology took the form of simple rankings of the so-called best colleges and universities in a country or area based on a series of supposedly commonsense indicators like "employer reputation," "academic reputation," and the presence of "international faculty and students," to name some of those used in academic rankings produced by magazines like the *Financial Times* for business schools and *U.S. News & World Report* for universities.[50] Rankings of research universities based on reputational measures and indicators of quality followed suit with the publication in 2003 of the so-called Shanghai Ranking of the top 1,000 universities of the world. Published each year, this ranking now competes with the QS World University Ranking and the *Times Higher Education* World University Ranking, also published annually.

Confronted with the many competing rankings, Joël Bourdin, a French senator, observed that each of them seems to have the unfortunate tendency of being biased in favor of different institutions: "The Shanghai Ranking favors American universities, while the Leiden ranking seems to have a certain bias towards Dutch universities."[51] He could have added to this list the École des Mines ranking, which sees French *grandes écoles* in a very flattering light, and yet they are marginal in the Shanghai ranking, all the while using as an indicator "the number of alumni holding a post of chief executive officer or equivalent in one of the 500 leading international companies." Given the intimate relations between French *grandes écoles* and France's large companies (many of them formerly state-owned), the chosen indicator inherently favors these institutions.[52]

Even before these rankings appeared on the market, the most systematic evaluation system for universities was the Research Assessment Exercise (RAE), established in the mid-1980s in the United Kingdom under Margaret Thatcher. The gigantic task of this system was to assess the research activities of all academic departments, in all disciplines, in all UK universities every four or five years, and judge the quality of research in the various departments (and therefore their publications in particular), with a peer-review committee producing a final grade. After the first evaluation of 1986, which assigned departments a score between 1 (national recognition) and 4 (world leader), the ranking has become even more differentiated to include intermediate levels (3a and 3b, for example) and higher levels (5 and 5*).

The incentive to take that evaluation seriously was that a portion of government budgets allocated to universities was attached to these scores, with the highest-rated institutions receiving larger grants.

The bureaucratic weight of this evaluation system is enormous to this day: fifteen sectors, divided into sixty-seven research areas. It mobilized approximately 1,500 evaluators.[53] The last assessment under this system was carried out in 2008, just to be redesigned and renamed the Research Excellence Framework (REF)—note the presence of the catchword *excellence*—and the results of this new system came out in 2014. As was the case with the RAE, the results affect the level of government subsidies distributed to universities. In fact, the procedure has changed little. Departments are ranked on five levels ranging from one to four "stars," plus one "unclassified" level for the weakest ones.[54] These procedures remain essentially based on peer judgments, site visits, and the analysis of the reports of activities written by the departments. The committee members judge the overall quality of research without really using any systematic bibliometric indicators. Although the production of publications is of course taken into account, it is part of an overall judgment that is ultimately qualitative.

This lack of systematic use of bibliometrics has been criticized given the large amount of time and money needed for going through the whole exercise. In response, a recent report analyzed the REF rankings and compared them with different bibliometric variables. Its basic conclusion is that "individual metrics give significantly different outcomes from the REF peer review process, showing that metrics cannot provide a like-for-like replacement for REF peer review."[55] Even limited to the use of a peer review committee, one could ask: What is the real merit (or "added value," to speak like managers) of an evaluation system that cost about 250 million pounds[56] and concludes that 75% of British universities are "internationally excellent (46%)" or "world leaders (30%)," with another 20% being "recognized internationally"?[57]

It is only in the mid-1990s that the integration of bibliometric data in university-funding formulas appeared in Australia, followed by Flanders, Belgium, in 2003.[58] In such a purely automatic quantitative system, evaluation is no longer aimed at improving practices and activities. Rather, it is used to sanction universities considered to be lesser performing (in light of the selected indicators) through budgetary measures. These allocation systems, which push institutions to increase the number of publications, have been heavily criticized by scientists.[59] In Australia, these criticisms led the government to abandon the original system in 2007 and replace it by another, based on peer review but "informed by a range of quantitative indicators."[60]

As could be expected, studies of the effects of research assessments based on the production of articles have shown that researchers adjust their behavior to meet the criteria used to evaluate them.[61] As Maya Beauvallet noted in her study of performance indicators used in public and private organizations under the influence of the New Public Management ideology: "any indicator, once built and installed, improves simply because we put the spotlight on it."[62]

Fortunately, organizations that mechanically integrate bibliometrics into funding formulas remain the exception, and they should not be imitated. After investigating ten countries on their use of bibliometric indicators in the funding formula of universities, the Council of Canadian Academies concluded its 2012 report by emphasizing that "mapping research funding allocation directly to quantitative indicators is far too simplistic, and is not a realistic strategy."[63] The 2015 report from the Higher Education Funding Council for England (HEFCE), *The Metric Tide*, came to a similar conclusion.[64]

Quantify to Control

The lively discussions surrounding the use of bibliometric indicators in the evaluation of researchers often overlook a fundamental aspect of evaluation: namely, the central role of the expertise of researchers in the assessment process. The willingness of many organizations to rank social sciences and humanities journals according to their supposed "quality" is in fact a way to mechanize the evaluation of papers in a kind of Taylorization of evaluation, aiming at a de-skilling of the expertise needed for such evaluations.

Although based on peer review rather than bibliometrics—which is not well adapted to humanities—journal rankings have predictable perverse effects for which their supposed usefulness cannot compensate. For example, once a journal has been ranked "A" by an obscure committee, it will tend to attract papers whose topics are inappropriate to the journal, which will lead to a higher rejection rate for reasons other than quality (not to mention the increased workload for the editors). Another predictable perverse effect is that such classifications will make it difficult for new journals to emerge and earn recognition, as authors will be reluctant to submit their papers to a journal that is not even ranked. Note also that the bureaucratic machinery will have to reassess rankings regularly to include new journals, thus generating a great deal of bureaucracy for doubtful results. The point is not to encourage the proliferation of journals, but to suggest that the choice of where to publish should be left to the members of the scientific community, as they can easily decide for themselves, at any given time, where their paper will get the most attentive reception given their subject matter.

Defining "International"

Another important but less obvious perverse effect of the use of journal rankings and IFs in research evaluation is that it turns researchers away from local, marginal, or unfashionable topics. This is especially dangerous in the humanities and social sciences, whose objects are inherently more local than those of the natural sciences. It is obvious that some subjects are less "exportable" than others. Since the most cited journals are published in English (a characteristic too often erroneously considered as being synonymous with "international journal"), access to them depends on the interest of these journals in the objects studied. An economist who wants to "maximize" its number of citations would thus tend to study the economy of the United States rather than that of France or Canada, which are of little interest to American journals of economics that happen to be the most cited.[65] A sociologist whose topic is "international," and thus delocalized, or who talks only of theory, is more likely to export papers than a colleague proposing an empirical study of a specific aspect of his own society.

Hence, a comparison of the German social theorists Jürgen Habermas and Niklas Luhmann, for example, flows smoothly into the international market of ideas, as it has no local empirical content that may diminish its appeal to an American sociological journal. And a study of the buying behavior in the south of France or Britain is likely to have more difficulty being published in international journals. But is it really less important to consider these local questions than to study more exportable topics, like the variations of the New York Stock Exchange?

There is, therefore, a real danger that local objects that are socially important will be undervalued and thus ultimately neglected if citation indicators are used mechanically, without taking into account their indexicality (the ethnomethodologist's term for the local roots of social sciences and humanities research objects). This phenomenon is not hypothetical and has already been measured in the case of Canadian economists who, over the last thirty years, have tended to lose interest in local economic problems in order to publish in the so-called top journals of their discipline.[66] In other words: there are no American "electrons," but there are "national economies" and even a "Bible belt culture," which are worth studying even though they are not international and thus will accrue fewer citations.

Not taking the ontologies of different disciplines into account in interpreting bibliometric indicators can only push researchers to abandon research on less fashionable topics for fear of not being able to publish in journals ranked "A" or "B" in official evaluation systems. Curiously enough, "A" journals in such classification schemes are mostly English-language, whereas national journals tend to be ranked "B," and so-called local ones are ranked "C" by coopted committees and organizations. In fact, it is hard not to detect a form of colonialism in many of the initial classifications proposed by the European organizations who produced these rankings of social science and humanities journals.[67] Indeed, if we rely only on total citations, it is almost inevitable that English-language journals will be better ranked, for the demographic reason that the potential number of readers in a given specialty is generally higher for English than for a foreign language such as French.[68] By contrast, this number says nothing about the international or national origin of these citations. This question is particularly important in the social and human sciences, for the reasons already discussed concerning the local nature of most social sciences and humanities research.

An initial indicator of the level of internationalization could be the geographical origin of the authors publishing in a given journal. On this basis, for example, we find that between 2000 and 2012, 81% of authors in the *American Journal of Sociology* were affiliated with American institutions, while the proportion of British authors in the *British Journal of Sociology* was only 61%, and its Canadian counterpart, *Canadian Journal of Sociology*, had 72% Canadian authors. The first is thus essentially an American, local journal, less international in its authorship than either of the other two.

Another useful way to measure the international visibility of these journals is to look at the language used by those who cite them. We find here again that 97% of the citations to the *American Journal of Sociology* come from English-language articles, which leaves only 3% coming from other languages. In contrast, the French social science journal *Actes de la recherche en sciences sociales* gets only 64% of its citations from Francophone sources, 26% from Anglophone sources, and more than 3% from German sources. The geographic origin of citations also shows greater local concentration for the *American Journal of Sociology*, with two-thirds of its citations coming from the United States, while only 40% of citations to *Actes de la recherche* come from France.[69] This shows that even though the total volume of citations to the American journal is ten times higher than that obtained by the French journal, this does not necessarily entail greater international influence.

Insensitive to these intricacies and the dangers of misusing indicators not fit-for-purpose, promoters of a mechanized quantitative assessment dismiss the qualitative dimension, considered "subjective," from the evaluation process in order to rely strictly on statistics that can then be used by evaluators from outside the research area. Thus, we face a paradox. The evaluation of a researcher requires the establishment of a committee of peers who know the area. These peers know, by definition, the good journals in their field and do not require a so-called official list of them established by outsiders who ranked them A, B, and C.

But what these rankings do make possible is for evaluators ignorant of a given research domain to claim to offer a legitimate evaluation simply using those lists. Their ignorance of the field should in fact have excluded them from the evaluation committee. Such mechanical rankings are part of a move from qualitative "peer review" to quantitative "expert review," which subtly shifts the ground from "peers" (that is, real experts in the field) to a more ill-defined "expert," who may in fact be no "peer" and no "expert" either, and thus needs crutches like journal rankings to evaluate researchers since they cannot themselves evaluate the content of the research being evaluated.

The proliferation of poorly constructed indicators contributes to transforming the usual evaluation process—based on real peer review—by transferring it into the hands of "experts" through a de-skilling process based on using standardized numbers that can be interpreted by any coopted "evaluator" who does not have to know the specific content of the research being evaluated. The fact that many researchers unconsciously contribute to the implementation of these rankings and to the use of invalid indicators does not change the fact that these methods have the objective effect of minimizing the role of qualitative assessment and of replacing it by mechanical evaluations that do not need any particular expertise. As such, evaluation moved from a skilled operation to an automated, mechanical one.

"Evaluating" Is Not "Ranking"

Ranking is often confused with evaluation. In fact, these two operations are quite different. Although rankings presuppose a kind of evaluation, the latter does not imply the former. As opposed to an evaluation, which aims at taking stock at some point in time of the state of the activities of an individual or an organization and is therefore directed first at the person or organization assessed, rankings are essentially a form of public advertisement. The very fact of making a ranking public is not insignificant for it can lead to potentially adverse and stigmatizing effects.

At this point, let's distinguish between official and unofficial rankings. All researchers have an intuitive ranking of journals in their own field of specialization. Some journals clearly have more prestige than others. But these loosely shared subjective ratings are flexible and vary among individuals in relation to their research specialty, which can be very narrow. The situation changes completely when such a pecking order becomes sanctioned through a self-appointed organization that publishes an "official" list that announces to everyone that one journal is "C" and another one "A," as if those rankings were based on taken-for-granted and generally accepted criteria of "excellence." Such formalization necessarily produces perverse effects that the implicit and informal rankings used by researchers in choosing where to publish do not generate. Researchers familiar with what is happening in their field know that they can find excellent papers in many journals that would be considered in some rankings as being "B" or "C." Informal exchanges between members of a scientific community allow flexible and nonstigmatizing evaluations, and there is no real need for regular and bureaucratic reevaluations of official rankings that, as we said before, aim at de-skilling the evaluation process.

We must admit, however, that the scientific community is itself often divided on these issues. Some researchers, in some disciplines, have decided to accept these official classifications of journals into A, B, and C categories. Other researchers and other disciplines have refused such a ranking, arguing that it is altogether arbitrary, and have suggested replacing it simply by a "scientific perimeter," a term defined to exclude only journals that are obviously not academic. This second approach avoids the trap of deciding which journal should be officially labeled A, B, or C, a process that obscures the arbitrariness of such choices, which are necessarily subject to power struggles and power relations between researchers.

The question is: Who exactly has the legitimacy to enact such a classification? Who uses the classification A, B, C? It is quite significant that all the major journals in the history and sociology of science were the first to collectively reject, in a common editorial published in 2009, the ranking of journals originally proposed by the European Science Foundation.[70] There is a struggle within any scientific field—it would be naive to ignore it—and a look at the composition of the various committees responsible for ranking journals in all areas of the human and social sciences suggests that the members of these committees are not always the most recognized researchers in their fields.

It seems that we are dealing here with what Pierre Bourdieu has called the "Zhdanov effect," after Andrei Zhdanov, the spokesperson for realist-socialist art under Joseph Stalin. According to Bourdieu, the dominated member of a scientific field is more likely to participate in an operation that can affect the mainstream actors in the field, even though doing so diminishes its autonomy.[71] Being one of those in charge of officially declaring which journal is ranked "A" and which "C" may indeed be exhilarating.

It is often said that rankings are inevitable and that we must live with them. This is false. The resistance of researchers is quite effective at blocking such misguided projects. In Australia, for example, the strong reaction of the scientific community against a proposed journal-ranking scheme forced the government to backtrack.[72] In France, too, the actions of many researchers compelled the organizations that promoted such a ranking to transform it into a simple list of journals by defining, as we noted previously, a scientific perimeter.[73] One can indeed define a set of journals considered scientific in a given field without falling into the trap of rankings that actually bypass peer control and replace it with mechanical decision making. The world of research has no reason to yield to external requirements whose logic is foreign to its internal norms.

Having now looked at the many perverse effects of using ill-defined indicators, it is time to suggest a set of well-defined criteria that should be used to distinguish the good from the bad indicators, thus diminishing the risk of using crooked thermometers to diagnose a fever. In other words, let us now try to evaluate evaluations.

4   The Evaluation of Research Evaluation

Over the last decade, much discussion has been devoted to the creation of "new indicators," essentially in the context of a policy demand for more thorough evaluation of research and higher education institutions. We have thus seen the multiplication of indicators—there are already dozens integrated in many existing rankings of universities. Whatever the reasons (given and analyzed in previous chapters of this book) for the excitement over "the metric tide" (to use the title of a recent report on the subject[1]), it raises a basic question that, curiously, has received scant attention in bibliometrics, as if all the energies devoted to the manufacture of new indicators left no time for a serious reflection about what exactly these indicators are measuring. This question is simply: Which criteria can tell us that a given indicator is valid and really measures what it is supposed to measure?

It is, of course, impossible to discuss all the indicators that have been proposed over the last ten years, and we will focus on the most popular, like the h-index that has already been discussed, as well as a few others used in university rankings.[2] What is most remarkable about the multiplication of indicators is that they are never explicitly submitted to any criteria to test their validity before they are used to evaluate researchers or universities. So, after having recalled some basic principles of research evaluation, and having discussed the various kinds of data that can be used to construct indicators aimed at evaluating scientific research, I will propose a set of criteria to assess the validity of any indicator that supposedly measures a given dimension of a concept.

As scientific director of the Observatory of Science and Technology (OST) at the University of Quebec at Montreal (UQAM), I have, over the past twenty years, worked with many organizations to conduct bibliometric evaluations of research institutions. Although it may seem surprising, it was frequently necessary to remind my clients that we cannot assess anything if we do not first identify the mission and objectives of the organization in question. Indeed, it should go without saying that (1) one cannot evaluate a government laboratory and a university research center in the same way, for they have different missions and thus need different measures of their activities; and (2) the evaluation must be undertaken in relation to previously determined goals. It is also imperative that these objectives be specific enough, because one must start from those objectives to define indicators that can measure whether these goals were achieved.

If the first mission of a government laboratory is to ensure the protection of citizens by carrying out various more or less routine measures of quality and security, it should be obvious that the number of publications or citations in scholarly journals is not the most important indicator of success. Conversely, a university research laboratory that gets plenty of industry contracts but publishes little in scientific journals could be considered problematic, given the usual core mission of a university, which is to increase knowledge, make it publicly accessible, and train students in all disciplines and professions. In other words, one should not first select indicators and then adapt the mission to them; rather, one should first establish the mission and goals and then try to find adequate indicators to measure the expected kinds of results achieved through the activities of the members of the organization.

Units of Measurement

In the field of higher education and research, despite repeated calls to multiply indicators, the basic units that can enter into any possible indicator remain relatively limited. On the input side, there are people (researchers, postdoctoral scientists, students, etc.), instruments, and money that generate activities. On the output side, one can tally the different products of these activities: publications (articles, books, reports), patents, conferences, and, of course, trained graduate students (MAs and PhDs). Finally, looking at the uses and effects of the different outputs, one can assess the outcomes and impact of these activities. For graduates, measuring their rate of employment and level of satisfaction makes sense, but using salary data is more of an issue since traders are usually better paid than scientists, but that in itself does not make them "better." To measure the use, visibility, impact, or quality of papers, one can count the citations that they get in other papers, or even in patents. In the Internet age, we can use new measures of visibility, such as the number of times the digital versions of the articles have been accessed or downloaded. Going further beyond the limit of the scientific field, one can also measure the visibility of papers in the public space by looking at the many Internet discussion platforms, like Twitter and blogs.[3]

Come to think of it, those variables are essentially the only units—often confused with metrics, as if any unit could serve to measure impact—that one can use to construct quantitative indicators for research evaluation, combining them in various ways to properly assess the different phases of research activities. Having identified the various possible units from which to construct indicators, and before asking what they really mean, we must look at the possible data sources to gain access to them in a practical manner.

Data Sources

It is one thing to identify indicators for an assessment; it is quite another to ensure that the data to construct them are available, reliable, and accessible at an affordable price. Existing databases on the inputs and outputs of scientific research are not always available in the required form. Hence, there is no global and easily accessible source of information on the total budgets allocated to research in all countries and in all universities, though the Organisation for Economic Co-operation and Development (OECD) does collect data on research and development (R&D) on the basis of the *Frascati Manual*. It is also very costly to gather such obvious data. What is true for budgets is also true for PhD graduates. Fortunately, global databases on the output of scientific publications exist, and despite their limitations, they are the basic sources for doing research evaluation.

Three major sources can now be used to measure the output and impact of scientific publications. The oldest, which has already been presented in some detail in chapter 1, is the Web of Science (WoS), by Thomson Reuters. Since 2004, it has had a competitor in Elsevier's Scopus database, as the oldest publishing company has understood that it could make good use of the thousands of journals that it disseminates covering most disciplines to build its own bibliometric database. Finally, there is Google Scholar, which also went online in 2004. While access to the first two databases is restricted to subscribers, Google Scholar is free (for now, anyway …). From the point of view of rigorous and transparent research evaluation, the major advantage of the first two sources is that their content is controlled and well defined, as one can know the list of journals included at any given time. The downside, of course, is that they are not free—in fact, they can even be quite expensive. While Google Scholar is free, and thus easily accessible to anyone, the problem is that its content is not well defined and varies constantly, so that we have no idea of its real content. Being based on the total content of the Internet, it includes peer-reviewed articles, but it also offers any other documents that one can put on a personal website. Items can appear and disappear as well, so one has no control over the validity of indicators calculated from this source. This is problematic from an ethical point of view, as evaluations should be transparent when they can affect people's careers. In addition, this database does not contain the institutional addresses of authors, which further limits its use for evaluation purposes. Not only that, but Google Scholar is vulnerable to manipulation.[4]

Cyril Labbé, a French computer scientist at Grenoble Joseph-Fourier University, showed how to manipulate the contents of Google Scholar to increase the h-index of a fictional researcher, whom he named Ike Antkare.[5] He created 100 short articles citing each other and placed them on a website. They were then harvested by Google Scholar, which generated an h-index of 94—a figure very difficult to achieve by most actual scientists.

Some have used this case to point out the limits of bibliometrics. In fact, however, it says nothing about bibliometrics per se, but rather about Google Scholar, which is not a reliable database for doing rigorous and ethically transparent bibliometric evaluation of an individual scientist. The trick used on behalf of Ike Antkare (decode as: "I can't care …") would not have been possible in the WoS or Scopus databases since the journals they cover publish peer-reviewed articles, not documents that simply happen to be on the Internet somewhere. And the fact that at the aggregate level, for large groups or institutions, there is a correlation between the results of various databases does not validate the use of Google Scholar, since for individual evaluations, the quality of the database and the sources that it contains is crucial to the credibility of the evaluation process and the correct interpretation of the indicators.

The data source used, therefore, is as important as the indicators themselves to ensure the quality and credibility of the evaluation process. The new market for research evaluation that has developed over the last ten years stimulated the creation of new firms specialized in evaluations and benchmarking based on their own private databases. Academics Analytics, for example, collect diverse information on university professors (like publications, citations, funding and awards), while Plum Analytics gather information on "citations, usage, mentions, captures, and social media."[6] They then use the results for doing evaluation under contracts with universities. At Rutgers University, for example, this approach has led to conflict with professors who questioned the quality and validity of the information used to evaluate them,[7] information and metrics on which they have no control. It is indeed problematic to evaluate people on the basis of a database whose exact content and quality are unknown.

These new market conditions have also increased the competition between Thomson Reuters and Elsevier, and directly influenced the very content of their databases. Until 2004, when Scopus hit the market, the Science Citation Index (SCI) was unique and dedicated to the idea of covering only the best journals of all disciplines, which were basically defined as the most cited journals. Confronted with the competition of Scopus, which highlighted the fact that it covers many more journals (an attractive feature for libraries), the WoS has increased the number of journals that it indexes. The coverage, and not just the so-called quality of the included journals, thus becomes a selling point and a good reason for libraries to subscribe. Scopus (as of 2015) lists about 22,000 journals, and WoS 12,000. If one includes conference proceedings and other sources, Scopus's tally rises to about 29,000 sources and WoS to 18,000. The two databases have more than 50% of their journals in common, but Scopus has a larger number of unique journals.[8]

Limitations of Bibliometric Indicators

As indicated in the previous chapter, the (more or less) local nature of objects studied by different disciplines is not without consequences for the validity of bibliometric indicators, given the limited coverage of some areas by the most widely used databases (WoS and Scopus). Thus, it is clear that the proportion of international collaborations cannot be used as a valid indicator of internationalization when the prevailing contributions are single-author articles, as is still the case in disciplines such as history and philosophy. Similarly, one cannot expect the same level of international collaboration in research on the northern agriculture of France as in the study of the distribution of black holes in the universe. These simple examples highlight the importance of understanding the nature of the data used, as well as the specificity of the disciplines and research topics to be assessed, in order to ensure that the chosen indicator is appropriate and valid. It should also be remembered that the extent of coverage of disciplines, specialties, and countries varies according to the database used.

Another obvious limitation of the use of bibliometrics in research evaluation is the fact that these databases do not cover all the journals in which researchers publish. This has been often emphasized by librarians who have documented the presence or absence of publications from their university laboratories in different databases.[9] Given the law of large numbers, the less the scale of analysis is aggregated, the less reliable the results and the more they must be interpreted with great caution. The strong tendency to uncritically consider these databases as unanalyzable "black boxes" leads many to forget the obvious fact that unrecorded works (especially those in languages other than English) are thus undervalued, although it has not been demonstrated that these papers are of lesser quality than those published in journals covered in databases like Scopus and WoS.

It is often (correctly) noted that books are not indexed in the WoS (or Scopus), but that statement is often confused with the (incorrect) one that citations to books are not included in these databases. Now, it is obvious that the WoS and Scopus do include all the books cited in the journal articles that they cover. And given that social sciences and humanities journals cite books more often than articles, it is unlikely that adding books to the database will significantly change the distribution of citations in these disciplines. It would be very surprising that a person who is little cited in journals would become widely cited in books in the same discipline, especially since books now tend to contain revised versions of already published papers. For these reasons, it is probably useless for evaluation purposes to invest in creating a separate Book Citation Index, as Thomson Reuters recently did. For it is not the absolute number of citations that is important, but the relative distribution and proportion of citations received in a given domain.

Bibliometric evaluation is basically a form of sampling, although it is obviously a skewed and not random form, as it excludes most local journals. Adding water (citations in books) to such a pool of citations in journals will raise the average level of water (total number of citations) but most likely will not change its overall composition. For example, country rankings of the overall production of papers are roughly the same in the Scopus and WoS databases despite the fact that they cover different journals, although significant variations may appear at lower scales of aggregation, like disciplines. Country analysis is also very much influenced by the strong English-language bias of the major databases, particularly in social sciences and humanities, a factor that makes their use in these fields very problematic.[10]

Given that citations have long been the only unit that could be used to measure scientific impact, it is unsurprising that they have remained the focus of attention. The many criticisms of citation analysis, coupled with the research evaluation fever and the transformation of the publication landscape from paper to Internet, have converged to give rise to a movement promoting alternative measures of impact, which produced the "Altmetrics Manifesto" in 2010. In addition to repeating the usual clichés about citations—that "influential work may remain uncited," that we "ignore the context and reasons for citation," etc.[11]—the promoters of the movement insist that it takes years to get cited. They thus implicitly accept the curious idea that we must know immediately what has had an impact or not, and that the most likely way to know this is to look at immediate Internet visibility on the new and rapidly multiplying discussion platforms. Beyond the fact that the supposed alternative metrics measure little more than a visibility that includes citizens and outsiders to the scientific field, the most obvious effect of this discourse is to create a new niche market to compete with the one monopolized by Elsevier and Thomson Reuters. New companies now try to insert themselves between the researchers who write papers and the journals that publish them in order to capture part of the value associated with measuring the impact of research, the term being left vague to exclude no possible "measure": Twitter, blogs, reference managers, aggregators of open-access papers, what have you.

Whatever the future of the myriad altmetrics that are now proposed on the evaluation market, their indicators should obey the same criteria as any classic indicator measuring a concept. At this time, we know that none of these supposedly alternative measures of impact have a definite meaning, and that none can seriously serve as a basis for decision making in higher education and research.[12] It is, for example, obvious that citations to a scientific paper takes years to accrue, whereas the number of tweets will peak after only a few days. There is no doubt, however, that the former provides a better measure of scientific impact than the latter.[13]

From a sociological point of view, Twitter is basically a tavern conversation on a global scale: it gives access to superficial discourse that until now has been confined (fortunately) within their walls. To anyone seriously concerned with measuring the effects of scientific research, it is worth recalling that the half-life of citations is measured in years, whereas the half-life of blogs is of the order of days (and that of tweets is measured in mere minutes).[14] What is the meaning of impact indicators that leave no trace after a few days? On the basis of these different time scales, it should be obvious that counting tweets cannot serve as a valid indicator of scientific impact, although studying the dynamic of exchanges on Twitter certainly can tell us interesting things about what kind of science excites citizens active on that media—and what does not.

A Multidimensional Universe

The most irritating aspect of current debates on the quantitative assessment of research is the tendency to sum everything up in a single figure. The simplistic nature of this approach becomes obvious when one observes that such a summation amounts to transforming a multidimensional space (whose dimensions are defined by the different indicators), into a zero-dimensional point (or at best a one-dimensional line), thus losing most of the information provided by the various axes. Only the inclusion of several indicators makes it possible to take into account the various dimensions of a concept, like that of the impact of research. Thus, the academic world may be primarily interested in the scientific impact of publications, but we cannot neglect other possible types of impacts for which it is more difficult to find valid indicators.

Think of the economic, societal, cultural, and environmental impacts of scientific research. Moreover, in the case of universities, research is only one of its missions (or functions), and the quality of education cannot be measured on the sole basis of research, with complete disregard for the environment in which students are trained (with elements such as access to professors, library resources, and quality of buildings). If one wants to measure these dimensions, one must avoid the "lamppost syndrome"—looking for keys in an area lit by a lamp rather than where the keys have actually been lost. It is, therefore, necessary to go beyond the easy availability of certain kinds of data and do case studies to assess all kinds of impacts using adequate indicators. It is a costly but necessary qualitative operation when one seeks to measure the various kinds of outcomes and impacts of scientific research in several areas of society.[15]

Evaluating Indicators

Until recently, the use of bibliometric indicators for evaluation was limited to experts because access to the WoS and Scopus databases was costly, and they were the only sources of bibliometric data. With the rapid development of the Web, the Internet can now be freely used to make bibliometric (and, by extension, webometric) evaluations and rankings. Freely accessible but uncontrolled data source such as Google Scholar have undoubtedly contributed to a certain degree of anarchy (others prefer to call it "democratization"[16]) in research evaluation, because users with some technical skill are now able to measure the quality or visibility of their research (or that of their competitors) by fashioning their own ad hoc indicators.

The number of such spontaneous (or perhaps *raw* is a better word) evaluation methods and impact indicators has exploded in recent years. This, in turn, has contributed to a chaotic state of affairs in academia, whereby no one really knows how to interpret these measures. Rankings circulate as "black boxes," presented as indisputable "facts" about individuals or institutions, and they are supposed to help policymakers and university administrators set research and academic priorities. This evaluation fever has resulted in rampant multiplication and misuse of faulty indicators. I have lost count of the letters to *Nature* and *Science,* and of blogs by scientists, who claim to be evaluating their colleagues or their institution. Scientists now flaunt their h-index, while universities fret over their position in the many competing rankings.

Among the many problems concerning research evaluation, one finds the thorny issue of evaluating the validity of rankings. Despite the numerous publications now devoted to analyzing and criticizing them, most critics have addressed the unintended consequences of their uses, but few have really dug into the indicators themselves except to point out their limits, thus stopping short of questioning their epistemological foundation—that is, whether these indicators really have any definite meaning and thus measure what they are supposed to measure. Before assessing the inevitable limits of any indicator, one must first ensure that it is valid and indicates what it is supposed to indicate. If not, then the chosen indicator is better characterized as irrelevant or misleading rather than limited, and should be replaced by another more appropriate one.

Using rankings based on faulty measurements could result in bolstering policies based on poorly analyzed problems. The lack of serious methodological reflection given to the question of the validity of each of the indicators used to concoct rankings has not stopped university managers from investing scarce resources in order to improve their position in their preferred ranking, though they, in fact, are ignoring what is really being measured. Most ranking schemes do not have any of the properties necessary for good indicators, and it would be foolhardy to use them as a guide for policymaking. It should also be noted that, in both cases, a single number is used for ranking and evaluating the quality and impact of the research performed by organizations and individuals, despite the obviously multidimensional nature of research.[17] It is worth repeating that the very existence (and persistence) of such biased indicators and rankings seem to be a consequence of the aforementioned unwritten "social law" that any number beats no number.

It is striking that among the large number of essays for or against rankings, and in papers promoting new measures of scientific activity, few take the time to discuss in detail the conditions under which an indicator can be taken as valid.[18] The "Berlin Principles on Rankings of Higher Education Institutions," for example, contains sixteen principles to which rankings should adhere. Among these, one finds that rankings should (1) have clearly defined goals, (2) be transparent regarding their methodology, (3) choose relevant and valid indicators, (4) clearly identify the weight assigned to different indicators (if used) and limit changing them, and (5) recognize the diversity of institutions. Note that only one of these principles specifies in very general terms that indicators should be chosen "according to their relevance and validity" and that "the choice of data should be grounded in recognition of the ability of each measure to represent quality and academic and institutional strengths." Finally, the producers of the indicator should be "clear about why measures were included and what they are meant to represent."[19] Given the actual properties of existing rankings, it is clear that this principle is rarely, if ever, applied seriously since most measures used are not fit-for-purpose since they do not compare the dynamic behavior of the indicator with the behavior of the concept to be measured.

Faced with a proliferation of indicators that tend to be used to justify policy changes in higher education and research, one must go beyond the vague appeal to relevance and validity, terms whose precise meaning is rarely made explicit. Other criteria for evaluating indicators are also invoked that relate to the quality of data sources (e.g., timeliness) or the transparency of the construction of the indicator[20], but they are not central to the question of validity per se. I will thus concentrate in the following discussion on criteria directly related to the internal validity of the indicator, evaluated through its relation to the properties of the concept that it is supposed to measure.

Although we have seen that *evaluation* is not synonymous with *ranking*, both operations require the use of indicators. I argued that the sources and quality of information used are important, but we must stress that the construction of a valid indicator is the first condition to be met. It is wrong to believe that the "choice of a particular indicator is only a question of convenience" and that only the quality of data really matters.[21] To be valid, an indicator must itself obey certain criteria, independent of the sources of data used to feed it, for one can have good data but bad indicators, as well as good indicators but bad data. I thus propose three criteria as necessary conditions for validity. These define the essential properties that a well-constructed indicator should possess in order to be considered valid:

1. Adequacy of the indicator for the object that it measures
2. Sensitivity to the intrinsic inertia of the object being measured
3. Homogeneity of the dimensions of the indicator

Essential Characteristics of a Good Indicator

By definition, an indicator is a variable that can be measured and that aims at faithfully representing a given concept, referring to the property of an object that one wants to measure.[22] Typical examples of such concepts and indicators are inflation, which measures changes in the price of goods over time, and gross domestic product (GDP), which measures the national economic production of a country. The indicator is not the concept itself, but a numerical representation used as a way of measuring how the reality behind the concept changes over time or place. Thus, the properties of the indicator should always be checked against the properties that the concept is assumed to have, based on intuition and prior knowledge of the object that has the properties that we want to measure or on an independent empirical measure of that concept. The indicator should thus be strongly correlated with what we presume to be the inherent characteristics of the concept that we want to measure using that specific indicator.

1.   Adequacy

The first property of a good indicator is that it must be fit-for-purpose—that is, correspond to the object or concept being evaluated. Are the results produced by the indicator of the correct order of magnitude, given what we already know about the object? Do they correspond to our intuition of the concept? For instance, the level of investment in R&D is a good first measure of the intensity of research activity in a given country. It refers to an investment, and this cannot be considered a measure of output and even less of quality. Likewise, the total number of scientific papers published by a given country provides a good measure of the volume of its public research output, but not of its industrial research, the results of which one does not expect to see published (although industrial research can also lead to publications).

Those two classic indicators are based on the basic intuition that the more money you put into a research system, the greater the likelihood that it will produce more output. This intuition is supported by the fact that we typically find a strong relation between the size of countries, as measured by their GDP and their total number of published papers. The money is translated into human resources and equipment, and it is intuitive that even though the relation is not linear, as there are always diminishing returns, more money should give rise to more papers because it makes possible the enrollment of more students, the hiring of more professors, and the purchase of more and better equipment. Therefore, we can say that we have a good grasp of the meaning of these indicators, which behave as one would expect.

Whereas indicators of production are relatively well understood, things become more complicated when we move to abstract concepts like the "quality" or "impact" of research, as opposed to sheer quantity. To measure the scientific impact of a given author or institution, one could conduct some type of survey, asking many experts what they think of the quality or scientific impact of the work of a given individual or institution, and then compute an average using a qualitative scale. This could serve as an indicator of perceived quality, although the subjective aspects of such evaluations and the danger of circularity—the "best" is the one that most so-called experts tend to say is the best—are difficult to control.

Despite its limitations, such a definition of the indicator is clear and makes sense, provided that the set of experts chosen corresponds to the domain being evaluated and is not entangled in conflicts of interest. Alternatively (and much less subjective and easier to implement), one could compute the number of citations received by a paper and use that figure as an indicator of scientific quality and impact; in this case, these two terms are taken as synonymous since both use the same indicator. More rigorously, one could also decide not to call this measure "quality" and use the more neutral term of "visibility": indeed, frequently cited papers are more visible than infrequently cited ones.

If one wants to associate citations with quality, then to keep from falling into a tautology, one must first test the connection between the concept (quality) and the indicator (citations) by finding a relationship between citations and an independent measure of quality, already accepted as a valid measure. In this regard, sociological and bibliometric studies since the 1970s have consistently shown that there is indeed a good correlation between how often an author is cited and how renowned he or she is, as measured by other indicators of eminence like important prizes and awards or academic nominations to scientific academies.[23] This relation is also consistent with our understanding of the role of recognition in scientific communities, which requires acknowledging previous work through citations.[24] An important caveat, however, is that indicators such as the number of published papers and citations obtained have mostly been validated in the case of the natural sciences, so one should not mechanically and blindly transfer their use to the social sciences or the humanities. One has to take into account differences between these disciplines—for example, the fact that in humanities, books are much more common than articles as a means of disseminating new results and are cited over a longer period of time.[25]

An example of an indicator that is not fit-for-purpose is the one based on the number of Nobel Prize winners associated with a given university. Although it is obvious that the Nobel Prize in itself can be taken as an excellent measure of the quality and scientific impact of the whole career of a researcher or scientist, a problem arises from the fact that this indicator measures work usually done decades earlier, which does not help one evaluate a university at the present time. Time being an important variable in the measure of an attribute, it should be obvious that taking into account the Nobel Prizes attributed for work done more than twenty years earlier to researchers associated with a given university shed no light on the quality of that institution today. Although that concept should be obvious to everyone, this indicator remains an important component of the Shanghai Ranking, which pretends to rank the best universities in the world.

Another example of lack of adequacy is the ranking of universities based on their presence on the Web, which does not measure anything definite beyond the mere fact that they exist on the Web, or when one defines the quality of a university by "counting all the external in-links that the University's web domain receives from third parties."[26]

2. Sensitivity

A major intrinsic characteristic of any object is its inertia—that is, its resistance to change—which thus affects the swiftness at which such changes can happen. Thus, a good indicator is one that varies in a manner consistent with the inertia of the object being measured, since different objects change with more or less difficulty (and rapidity) over time. Consider a digital thermometer (instead of the older mercury-based thermometer). If, in a given room (with no drafts), we first measure a temperature of 20 degrees and then, a minute later, 12 degrees and five minutes after that, 30 degrees, common sense would lead the observer to conclude that the instrument is defective, not that the temperature of the room is varying that wildly. We know very well that its temperature cannot change that much in the space of three minutes with no heat on or door or window opened.

Now take the case of universities. It is well known that large academic institutions are like supertankers—they cannot change course quickly (and thankfully so, because this allows them to avoid responding to shortsighted or frivolous so-called social demands[27]). Therefore, an annual ranking where an institution moves in a single year from, say, twelfth to eighteenth or twelfth to ninth, should strongly suggest that the indicator showing that movement is defective, not that the quality of the institution has plummeted or risen significantly during the year.

Given the inevitable variance in the data from one year to the next, it is clear that most annual changes in positions are random and devoid of any real significance. For this reason, it does not really make sense to measure (or evaluate) them every year. In the United States, for instance, the National Research Council produces a ranking of all doctoral programs at all American universities in every discipline, but it does so only once every ten years[28]. Why choose such a low frequency? Simply because, in addition to the high costs associated with conducting such an evaluation properly, the probability of a given academic program being "excellent" in 2008 but "mediocre" in 2009 is very small, if one excludes a sudden wave of retirements. This time scale thus respects the fact that universities are relatively inertial institutions. It also suggests that evaluating large research groups every two or three years makes little sense (and constitutes a waste of resources), and that doing so every six to eight years (or ten, even) might be a more realistic and economical way of observing real changes.

In light of this analysis, one can conclude that annual rankings of universities, be they based on surveys, bibliometrics, or webometrics, have no foundation in methodology and can only be explained by marketing strategies on the part of the producers of these rankings. They serve no serious scientific purpose and may even have negative unintended consequences if used by academic managers who think they should adjust the priorities of their institutions to fit the latest wave of indicators.

3. Homogeneity

A third crucial property that any valid indicator should possess is being homogeneous in its composition. With respect to research, homogeneous indicators of research output (say, at the level of a country) can be constructed using the number of articles published in leading scientific journals. Indicators based on papers can help construct a descriptive cartography of research activities using input and output measures. In addition, one can obtain a productivity index from the input/output ratio. However, if one were to somehow combine the number of papers with a citation measure—as does, for example, the h-index (more on that later in this chapter)—one would then obtain a heterogeneous indicator. The problem is the same with all indicators that combine, arbitrarily, different kinds of indicators like "academic reputation" and "international faculty and students." The fundamental methodological problem with such heterogeneous composite indicators is that when they vary, it is impossible to have a clear idea of what the change really means, since it could be due to different factors related to each of its heterogeneous parts.[29] One should always keep each indicator separate and represent it on a spiderweb diagram, for example, in order to make clear the various components of the concept being measured.

To these three basic criteria should be added another one that is most often implicit, but should be made explicit, as it can also help to eliminate flawed indicators: namely, the indicator must be a monotonically increasing function of the concept that it measures. That means that if the value of the concept is higher, the value measured by the indicator must also be higher. Moreover, all the values of the indicator must remain consistent with the meaning of the indicator. That is obvious in the case of temperature: a million degrees is still a temperature, and it is hotter than a hundred degrees. This, however, is often not the case for many indicators used in existing university rankings.

A single example should suffice to show the importance of the monotonic relation between concept and indicator. Among the many measures used to rank universities, some include the proportion of foreign students and professors as an indicator of "success on the world stage."[30] But for that measure to be a good indicator of success, the higher the value, the better it should be. Thus, a university with 90% of foreign professors would be considered better than one with only 20% of them. Now, given that the social mission of public universities is first to contribute to the development of the local society (or state, or country), it seems pretty obvious that a country whose universities cannot produce local professors is a colonial institution. Thus, the proportion of foreign professors (or students, for that matter) is not in itself an adequate measure of the success or attraction of an institution. The point is not, of course, to deny the value of having international students or professors in any given university, but simply to stress the fact that such a number is not a *valid* indicator of the concept to be measured. One could argue that a university is "good" only if it has between say

15% and 25% of foreign professors, but such a choice is obviously arbitrary and has no foundation in the concept to be measured. Moreover, there is no need of such an indicator if its validity is limited to a very small portion of its possible range.

Let us now use these criteria to analyze more carefully a widely used ranking of universities (the Shanghai Ranking) and a very popular indicator of the quality of individual research (the h-index). These two cases offer examples of indicators constructed at different levels of aggregation: the Shanghai Ranking evaluates institutions, while the h-index focuses on individuals. At this point, however, the reader may already suspect that these two measurements do not constitute valid indicators, and scientists and policymakers promoting them as "objective" and "international" measures should think twice before using them as a sound basis of evaluations and decision making.

Invalidity of the Shanghai Ranking and the H-Index

The Shanghai Ranking is computed by summing six different measures. The first four, worth 20% each, involve the number of:

1. Faculty members who have received a Nobel Prize or the Fields Medal (for mathematics)
2. Researchers at the institution who are on the "most cited" list compiled by Thomson Reuters
3. The institution's papers that are published in *Nature* and *Science*
4. Articles found in the WoS

Two additional measures, worth 10% each, round out the indicator:

The number of alumni who have received a Nobel Prize or the Fields Medal
An adjustment of the five preceding indicators based on the size of the institution

Clearly, the final index is not adequate since it is a composite of several heterogeneous measures: the number of publications in *Science* and *Nature* is not commensurate with the number of Nobel Prizes. What is even more surprising is that the results on which the final rankings are based turn out to be very difficult to reproduce.[31] One could also question the adequacy of an indicator such as "the number of articles in *Science* and *Nature*," given that these two journals do not cover all disciplines and, moreover, are heavily biased in favor of the United States. In 2004, for example, 72% of the articles in *Science* and 67% in *Nature* had at least one author with an address in the United States. Most important, given what we know about the inertia of universities, we should certainly cast doubt on an indicator that causes universities—for instance, the Free University of Berlin and Humboldt University—to move up (or down) almost 100 places simply by being associated (or not) with Albert Einstein's 1922 Nobel Prize. One might also wonder whether the quality of a university really depends on the research conducted on its campus many decades earlier.[32] Consequently, it does not meet our sensitivity criterion either.

To show how the rankings can go against what we otherwise generally know about universities, let us take the case of Canadian universities compared with French ones. In the 2009 Shanghai Ranking of the best universities in the social sciences, we observe that among the top 100, one finds eight Canadian universities but no French universities. Now, does anyone really believe that French social science is that much worse than Canadian social science? Of course not—and this bizarre result is simply an artifact of the data used, which are strongly biased against the European social sciences because papers written in French and German journals are underrepresented.[33] Therefore, using this ranking as a guide can only produce poor decisions, as most of the indicators used to construct it do not meet our basic criteria of validity. More recent university rankings (like the CWTS Leiden Ranking and U Multirank), are much better than the Shanghai ranking because they do not combine heterogeneous indicators with arbitrary weights, and they use well-defined indicators.[34]

If we now turn briefly to another fashionable indicator, the h-index, which I already analyzed in chapter 3, it obviously does not meet our validity criteria. Mixing the number of papers with the number of citations produces a heterogeneous indicator. Moreover, this index is not a strictly increasing function of the measure of the concept, as it should be, for, as we have seen, a lower index often hides a better-quality researcher. It does not measure quality, for it is very highly correlated with the quantity of papers published. Moreover, as noted in the previous chapter, its value never goes down over time. A thermometer with such weird behavior would not sell. And given that a good indicator must retain its intuitive relation to the concept that it seeks to measure, the various attempts to try to correct its deficiencies by inventing even less intuitive and more complicated indexes are doomed to failure, for such operations only make an invalid indicator even less intuitive and transparent.

Why Are Invalid Indicators Used?

Given this analysis, it is astonishing that so many university presidents and managers lose all critical sense and seem to take rankings at face value. Only a psychosociological analysis of managers and administrators would explain the appeal of a grading system that has no scientific basis. Undoubtedly, the rhetoric surrounding the globalization of the university market has exacerbated the sensitivity surrounding evaluation issues. Universities are now eager to attract foreign students in order to compensate for demographic decline or insufficient government subsidies and to jump on the internationalization bandwagon, albeit at the cost of neglecting their local duties.

There are exceptions, of course, and the president of the University of Toronto, commenting in 2006 on *Maclean's* magazine's annual ranking of universities, admitted that "Canadian universities have been complicit, en masse, in supporting a ranking system that has little scientific merit because it reduces everything to a meaningless, average score." And he added: "My institution has found Maclean's [ranking] useful for one thing only: Marketing. None of us really believes that the ranking has much intellectual rigor."[35] One also must take into account the transformation of the kind of people who now tend to run universities. As more and more nonacademics take the reins of higher education institutions, they seem to be more responsive to market forces, "branding," and the search for money than to academic principles and values. And it is certainly significant that managers are particularly fond of gurus selling their changing buzzwords.[36]

The lack of critical thinking on the part of many university administrators about the various rankings can even lead to ridicule, as shown by the sudden presence of Alexandria University in Egypt among the top research-intensive universities in the 2010 QS World University Ranking. The university boasted of its new status on its website, and the editor of the *Times Higher Education* magazine wrote to the university, saying that "any institution that makes it into this table is truly world class."[37] None of them asked the obvious question: How could an institution move in a single year from virtually unknown to world class? Fortunately, informed people were a little more skeptical. A year later, the QS ranking put Alexandria in position "601+," and the data for the year 2010 disappeared, leaving a blank instead of the original position, "147." Furthermore, since 2013, it has been ranked at position "701+."[38] Given the volatility of the positions and the arbitrary nature of selected indicators and weights, one can only smile at hearing the French minister of research seriously comment on the 2013 Shanghai ranking that despite the many reservations that she has about the value of this ranking, she was happy to note that French universities "nibble at a few places" on the list.[39] These examples should be enough to caution university managers to look inside the black box of ranking instead of taking that box as a welcome gift.

There are also political reasons that bad rankings still get used. As the case of France clearly shows, ranking systems can be used as a means of justifying university reforms. Given the priorities of the Nicolas Sarkozy government following his election in 2007, we can confidently assume that had French universities placed highly in the Shanghai Ranking, it would have been much more difficult for the president to justify his policies, and the government would have had a very different perspective on such rankings, probably dismissing them as not representative of the French university system that they wanted to reform. On the other hand, the ranking would have been used by those opposed to the reform as proof that French universities were in fact excellent and should be left alone.

Although many critics of evaluation and rankings point to administrators as the culprits, it is important to emphasize that, contrary to the belief that only managers seek to promote indicator-based evaluations, the rapid proliferation of the h-index within scientific disciplines has been largely a grass-roots phenomenon. Indeed, scientists themselves are often the ones who succumb to the anarchic uses of raw bibliometrics. As members of committees and boards with the power to affect policy decisions, they frequently push for the generalized use of such indicators, even though they have not tested their properties. This development only confirms that for scientists, the "enemy" is more often one's colleague than a distant bureaucrat.

How to Boost Your Ranking

An important contributory factor to the rise of rankings is the role played
by the communications and marketing divisions of universities, which
tend to see their institutions simply as a "product" to be sold using the
standard rhetoric of marketing. One can understand the reaction of university managers to the rankings if one notes that they are mainly used in
marketing strategies. Since at least the 1990s, the OECD has promoted a
global market for higher education, and the emergence of global rankings
in the early 2000s is part and parcel of this neoliberal current, which has
pushed universities to behave as if they were part of a global economic
market like any other "industry." But those who talk about "markets" also
talk about "competition" and, above all, "marketing," and we observe that
universities employ more and more so-called experts in communications to
burnish, renew, and sell their public image. Eleanor S. Abaya, communications director at a Canadian university, thus considers that it is time that
academics understand that we live in a market economy and that universities have to brand themselves to sell their products to potential buyers—
that is, the students. She explains that in much less time than expected, she
transformed the image of her institution into a "can-do university" where
one finds "top-notch research" (using typical buzzwords that sound good
and never have more than two syllables as modifiers).[40]

In contrast with this optimistic view of marketing, I see a different,
darker face of marketing when it is applied to universities. When I pay
close attention to product advertisements in newspapers, on TV, and now
at the movies, I'm always struck by how the carefully chosen language and
images stay just on the safe side of the line separating truth from lies. No
doubt, an army of lawyers went over the text and images to make sure that
nobody could object to their content, despite the obvious fact that their
effective message often clearly suggests what they say they do not want to
suggest. For example, automobile makers now target very young drivers
(aged 18–25) as potential clients. Their ads show cars appearing to move
faster than any legal speed limit in existence. But no problem: very small
print, shown for about 10 seconds during the clip, insists that "one should
not attempt to do the same," since what the viewer sees was done with
"expert drivers in special circumstances."

The problem with applying car-and-beer marketing techniques to universities is that the latter are supposed to search for truth, whereas car and beer sellers just want to make money. And business ethics is not the same as ethics in a university context, given the unique moral mission of the latter. Marketing can thus be a slippery slope for universities that want to advertise that they are "first" in something. They try hard to find a ranking in which they can be among the top. Many examples exist of universities using a ranking to boost their visibility, even when they know it has no scientific value.

Here is how it works. University X (I omit the real name to obviate shame and/or legal pursuit) found a ranking that it liked, but it probably did not want to reveal its *precise* position in it. Therefore, the local marketing expert chose the following sentence: "University X is *among the first five* universities in Canada." But why not simply mention its rank? Was it first? Certainly not, as it would have been proud to say "university X is *first* in ranking Z." Probably not second either, for the same reason. This leaves ranks 3, 4, and 5. I suggest that X probably ranked fourth or fifth, and the marketing reasoning was: we would like to be first, so let us put the word *first* in the sentence so that the reader may remember only that word after having seen the ad. Thus, let's say our university was "among the *first* five …" There is no law against this, although it stretches the limits of intellectual honesty in the way that many sellers of used cars and other dubious products do. I think that this kind of behavior slowly corrupts universities by promoting cynicism.

In another real-life example, University B, which seems to take world university rankings seriously even though they change each year in a manner inconsistent with the nature of university activities, was proud to announce that it was ranked twentieth. But it didn't mention that the year before, in the very same ranking, it was twelfth. Now, either the ranking means something, and twentieth position represents a dramatic drop in quality that should be followed urgently by a major reform and the resignation of its president or vice president of research, or the ranking is bogus, and twentieth is not better than ninetieth, and marketing should not be based on these numbers.

But cynicism seems to be dominant, for I often heard from high-ranking administrators: "Yves, you're right about these rankings, but we must use simple messages." As if it were not possible to promote universities honestly by presenting really important findings related to their basic missions (teaching and research)—prizes won by professors and students from peers and recognized experts. However, this task will remain difficult so long as promotional plans are left in the hands of marketing people who, attending a university's fair, have been trained to see only "the frenzy of both the 'sellers' and the 'buyers' and to witness the innovative promotional approaches that institutions are attempting as they become more competitive about marketing their brand."[41] By contrast, any true academic leader visiting the same fair would rather see curious and excited future university students discussing with professors and other students the different programs they're interested in, nervously trying to make an enlightened choice among them. The future of universities could well depend on how we decide to view what they were really doing in this fair.

Institutions that focus too much on their positions in rankings can even try to manipulate the data, much as editors of academic journals tried to manipulate their impact factor (IF) to improve their position in journal rankings (as we have seen already). It has been proven, for example, that several US institutions have doctored their data on certain indicators to improve their position in the *U.S. News & World Report* ranking.[42] This brings us to the ugly part of research evaluation.

Dummy Affiliations

The kind of intellectual corruption engendered by the ranking race is probably at its worst when academic institutions contact highly cited researchers who are employed by other institutions and invite them to add their address in their publications—in return for remuneration. These dummy affiliations, with no serious teaching or research tasks attached to them, allow marginal institutions to easily improve their position in the rankings of universities without having to create true laboratories. And researchers who participate in such trade are, of course, as guilty as the institutions. It may be considered ironic that bibliometrics can be used to identify ethically problematic behavior on the part of researchers and universities.

Since the magazine *Science* has shown that "Saudi universities offer cash in exchange for academic prestige," we can look in more detail at the actors in that game.[43] The publication by Thomson Reuters of a list of Highly Cited Researchers (HCRs) and their institutions provides much more interesting data than simply who are the most cited and which institutions hire them.[44] By providing data on secondary affiliations, this list inadvertently confirms the traffic in institutional affiliations that are used to boost institutions' places in world university rankings. The 2014 HCR list contains 3,215 researchers. Of these, only 707—about 22%—have more than one affiliation, as registered by them in their papers. Note that having more than one affiliation makes sense since one can put more than one address on a paper (department, affiliated hospital, research center, etc.). When we look at all the data in Thomson Reuters' WoS, we find that about 18% of authors in biomedical sciences put more than one address in their byline, as opposed to 11% in science and engineering and 10% in social sciences and only 6% in humanities. In these cases, however, one would expect that most of these secondary affiliations would be in the same country as the first address. This is indeed the case—only between 2% and 4% of authors with more than one address have their second address in a country different than the first. Interestingly, but as could be expected on the basis of international scientific recognition, the situation is quite different among highly cited authors. The HCR data shows that among the 707 researchers with more than one institutional affiliation, 296 (or 42%) have a foreign country as their second address; that's about ten times more than usual.

Another interesting piece of data is the frequency of the foreign institutions that turn up as the secondary addresses of these researchers. Focusing on institutions that appear at least ten times, we notice that the most "attractive" foreign institution by far is King Abdulaziz University (KAU) in Saudi Arabia, with 130 foreign authors. It is no surprise, then, that this university was the institution singled out in a *Science* magazine 2011 News Focus article as using foreign scientists to bolster its position in university rankings. On the other hand, a scientific powerhouse such as Harvard University has only 26 foreign affiliations as the second address in this list of highly cited researchers—far less than KAU. If we look at countries instead of institutions, the conclusion is the same: Saudi Arabia seems the most attractive for HCR, with 134 affiliations, followed by the United States, with only 32, and then the United Kingdom, with 19.

It seems quite clear that the very fact that these scholars put KAU as an institutional address in their paper placed that institution among the highly cited universities. As shown in table 4.1, Saudi Arabia has 134 (82%)

Table 4.1
Countries of Primary and Secondary Addresses of HCRs in 2014

Highly cited country	Number of HCRs	Primary address in that country	Secondary country different from primary one	% of external HCRs
Saudi Arabia	163	29	134	82
South Africa	13	8	4	31
Denmark	38	26	7	18
Finland	18	14	3	17
Singapore	20	15	3	15
Australia	99	73	12	12
Sweden	33	28	4	12
Austria	26	18	3	12
South Korea	27	19	3	11
China	174	144	16	9
Spain	57	44	5	9
Ireland	13	12	1	8
Italy	63	49	4	6
France	116	83	7	6
United Kingdom	350	304	19	5
Netherlands	97	77	5	5
Germany	185	162	7	4
Japan	125	99	3	2
Belgium	42	33	1	2
Canada	101	87	2	2
United States	1,927	1,698	32	2
Switzerland	75	67	1	1

of its 163 researchers on the HCR list with that country as a second, not first, address, and only 29 of them put Saudi Arabia as the first address. By contrast, most researchers—that is, more than 90%—from highly developed countries like the United States, United Kingdom, Germany, France, and Canada have their first address in their native country, as should be expected.

Intellectual Fraud?

All these data certainly suggest that some institutions seem to have discovered a cheap way to be considered excellent in world university rankings. But the same data also suggest that some highly cited researchers have
found an easy way to get more money in exchange for transferring some
of their symbolic capital to a university other than the one that employs
them full time. This is not a problem when the institutions are really committed to the researchers and offer them a real job that allows them to contribute directly to research and teaching that their students can enjoy. It is
quite another thing when the goal is simply to improve the position of an
institution in a ranking by artificially inflating the number of publications
in targeted scientific journals. Business schools—which have to maintain
their accreditation—are also fond of touting their place in various rankings.
Some of them are thus doing the same kind of strategic maneuvering—
adding foreign scholars to their list to make themselves look better by offer-
ing handsome premiums based on the ranking of the journals in which
their authors publish. In Europe, many institutions thus maintain a list
of hundreds of journals evaluated at between zero and 20,000 euros per
article.

These practices of "optimization" even affect the content of academic
research. In France, the newspaper *L'Etudiant* has shown that IPAG, a
French business school, has found a way to move up the rankings by focusing their publications on middle-rank journals and on topics favored by
those journals. With the evaluation criteria being based on the number
of stars obtained for each publication, one can focus on a top journal and
get 5 stars for one paper, or publish five articles in a 1-star journal. In any
event, $1 \times 5 = 5 \times 1$! A researcher from IPAG has candidly explained the
scheme: "We have identified journals more accessible than others. We try
to write papers that correspond to their expectations." He adds that they
do not waste time collecting original empirical data; rather, they focus on
existing sources that they can buy to facilitate fast publication. Responding
to colleagues from other institutions, who found this behavior problematic,
another IPAG member replied that they have not created the "rules of the
game"—they just exploit them to maximize their output.[45]

It should not come as a surprise to learn that business and management
school professors and administrators, who are knowledgeable in the field

of commerce, have learned to monetize their symbolic capital. But given the central place of accreditation systems in business school strategies, it is ironic that the EFMD Quality Improvement System (EQUIS) accreditation criteria also include the ethics of business schools, affirming that "The School should have a clear understanding of its role as a 'globally responsible citizen' and its contribution to ethics and sustainability."[46] One wonders if the blatant manipulations used to rise in the rankings do not in fact constitute a kind of intellectual fraud, or at least unethical behavior that is incompatible with the mission of an institution of higher education.

Institutions that take seriously their position in the many rankings that circulate through the academic marketplace do not always seem aware of the unintended and perverse consequences that they can generate, including the ironic result that some of their own researchers conspire to improve the position of their "competitors" by surreptitiously adding foreign addresses to their papers. If we cannot count on the moral fiber of university managers to put an end to this ethically dubious gaming on the basis of principle, we may be certain that they will act when they understand that some of the researchers whom they pay full time to make their own institutions famous are in fact "double agents" who will help their competitors to upgrade their own positions in the rankings—for a much reduced price. Thus, after university managers have worked so hard to encourage researchers to put the right institutional address on publications clearly, so that the symbolic benefits are attributed to their own institutions, it seems that the very abuses of research evaluation will now force those same institutions to verify the traffic of such addresses on these publications.

Conclusion: The Universities' New Clothes?

The many debates surrounding the question of the validity of various rankings of universities, as well as indicators of research impacts that now circulate throughout the academic world, amply demonstrate that these uses are determined by political and strategic reasons. Nonetheless, it remains somewhat mysterious that many otherwise intelligent and well-educated academics and administrators continue using invalid indicators, often called *metrics,* to promote their institutions and make important strategic decisions on hiring and promotions.

Such a situation seems curiously very much analogous to the one described by the nineteenth-century Danish author Hans Christian Andersen in his famous tale "The Emperor's New Clothes."[1] One may seriously wonder if by naivety or cynicism, many academic leaders and managers who take seriously these rankings are not in a position similar to that poor emperor, "who was so excessively fond of new clothes" that he had been persuaded by "two rogues, calling themselves weavers" that "they knew how to weave stuffs of the most beautiful colors and elaborate patterns." The new clothes "have the wonderful property of remaining invisible to everyone who was unfit for the office he held, or who was extraordinarily simple in character."

Although skeptical—for he could not see the supposed new cloth—but afraid of appearing stupid, the emperor's old minister, who was asked to monitor the work of the weavers, told them he would "tell the Emperor without delay, how very beautiful" he found the (in fact invisible) patterns and colors of his new suit—much the same as institutions buy rankings that they know to be highly problematic but are forcefully promoted by convincing sellers. Seeing nothing either, but also afraid of losing his "good, profitable office," another employee "praised the stuff he could not see, and declared that he was delighted with both colors and patterns." He confirmed to the emperor that "the cloth [the ranking!], which the weavers are preparing, is extraordinarily magnificent." The emperor thought he would show himself to be a fool, and not fit for his position, if he said aloud what he thought: that there was nothing to see. He thus preferred to say aloud, "Oh! the cloth [ranking] is charming. It has my complete approbation" and he agreed to wear it for the next procession (er, marketing campaign...).

During his public wandering, "all the people standing by, and those at the windows, cried out, 'Oh! How beautiful are our Emperor's new clothes! What a magnificent train there is to the mantle; and how gracefully the scarf hangs!' In short, no one would allow that he could not see these much-admired clothes; because, in doing so, he would have declared himself either a simpleton or unfit for his office." But then, there emerged "the voice of innocence," that of a little child in the crowd, who cried: "But he has nothing at all on!" The crowd finally repeated that obvious truth, and the emperor "was vexed, for he knew that the people were right; but he thought the procession must go on now! And the lords of the bedchamber took greater pains than ever, to appear holding up a train, although, in reality, there was no train to hold."

The question is whether university leaders will behave like the emperor and continue to wear each year the "new clothes" provided for them by sellers of university rankings (the scientific value of which most of them admit to be nonexistent), or if they will listen to the voice of reason and have the courage to explain to the few who still think they mean something that they are wrong, reminding them in passing that the first value in a university is truth and rigor, not cynicism and marketing.

We can also decide not to leave these decisions solely in the hands of academic leaders and work collectively to counter the forces that seek to impose illusory rankings on universities whose effects are more negative than positive, by continuing to make rigorous criticism of such practices each time they are used. Even if there may be no such thing as the inherent force of true ideas, it remains the case that reasoned critiques are more likely to defeat the most perverse uses of benchmarking than is the resigned acceptance that they are inevitable and that it is useless to oppose them.

Although bibliometric methods are essential to go beyond local and anecdotal perceptions and to map comprehensively the state of research and identify trends at different levels (regional, national, and global[2]), the proliferation of invalid indicators can only harm serious evaluations by peers, which are essential to the smooth running of any organization. Critical analysis of improvised indicators and rankings recalls that the devil is always in the details and that the road to hell is paved with good intentions. We must go beyond the generalities of those who repeat ad nauseam that "rankings are here to stay"—without ever explaining why this must be so—and open these "black boxes" in order to question the nature and value of each and every indicator used to assess research at a given scale[3]. Only these rational and technical analyses will ensure that decisions are based on solid evidence. Before attempting to rank a laboratory or a university among "the best in the world," it is necessary to know precisely what "the best" means, by whom it is defined, and on what basis the measurement is made. Without this conception of the nature and consequences of the measurement, the university captains who steer their vessels using bad compasses and ill-calibrated barometers risk sinking in the first storm.

Notes

Introduction

1. Many books have been published on these transformations of research and higher education. Here are some on my bookshelf, listed in chronological order: Bill Readings, *The University in Ruins* (Cambridge, MA: Harvard University Press, 1997); Sheila Slaughter and Larry L. Leslie, *Academic Capitalism: Politics, Policies, and the Entrepreneurial University* (Baltimore, MD: Johns Hopkins University Press, 1997); Abélard, *Universitas calamitatum: Le Livre noir des réformes universitaires* (Broissieux: éd. du Croquant, 2003); Christophe Charle and Charles Soulié (eds.), *Les Ravages de la modernisation universitaire en Europe* (Paris: Syllepse, 2007); Franz Schultheis, Marta Roca i Escoda, and Paul-Frantz Cousin (eds.), *Le Cauchemar de Humboldt: Les réformes de l'enseignement supérieur européen* (Paris: Raisons d'Agir, 2008); Claire-Akiko Brisset (ed.), *L'Université et la recherche en colère: Un mouvement social inédit* (Broissieux: éd. du Croquant, 2009); Derek Bok, *Universities in the Marketplace: The Commercialization of Higher Education* (Princeton, NJ: Princeton University Press, 2009); Sheila Slaughter and Gary Rhoades, *Academic Capitalism and the New Economy: Markets, State, and Higher Education* (Baltimore, MD: Johns Hopkins University Press, 2009); Peter Dahler-Larsen, *The Evaluation Society* (Stanford, CA: Stanford University Press, 2012); Stefan Collini, *What Are Universites For?* (London: Penguin, 2012). The list cannot be exhaustive, though, as books continue to appear on this topic.

2. Ivar Bleiklie, "Justifying the Evaluative State: New Public Management Ideals in Higher Education," *Journal of Public Affairs Education* 4, no. 2 (1998): 87–100; Margit Osterloh and Bruno S. Frey, "Academic Rankings between the "Republic of Science" and "New Public Management," in *The Economics of Economists: Institutional Setting, Individual Incentives, and Future Prospects*, ed. Alessandro Lanteri and Jack Vromen (Cambridge, MA: Cambridge University Press, 2014): 77–103.

3. Each discipline seems to discover the same questions while at the same time forgetting about previous debates in neighboring fields. After having been limited to specialized journals in scientometrics, bibliometrics is now discussed in many disciplinary journals, especially biomedical journals. In France in particular, where

intellectual debates are unusually vigorous, many academic journals have devoted thematic issues to the question of research evaluation over the last seven years: examples include *Le Débat*, no. 156 (2009); *L'Homme et la société*, no. 178 (2010) ; *Communication et organization*, no. 38 (2010); *Connexions*, no. 93 (2010); *Quaderni*, no. 77 (2012); *Esprit* (July 2012); *Mouvements*, no. 71 (2013); see also Albert Ogien, *Désacraliser le chiffre dans l'évaluation du secteur public* (Versailles: Quae, 2013).

4. Benoît Floc'h, "Le classement de Shanghaï affole les universités pas les étudiants," *Le Monde*, August 15, 2015; see also Joël Bourdin, *Rapport d'information fait au nom de la délégation du Sénat pour la Planification sur le défi des classements dans l'enseignement supérieur.* Appendix to the minutes of the July 2, 2008 meeting, p. 98; accessed December 21, 2015, http://www.senat.fr/rap/r07-442/r07-4421.pdf. The data come from a 2015 survey of 600 students from 46 countries on five continents; see *Les notes Campus France*, May 2015; accessed December 21, 2015, http://ressources.campusfrance.org/publi_institu/agence_cf/notes/fr/note_47_fr.pdf.

5. Blaise Cronin and Cassidy Sugimoto (eds.), *Bibliometrics and Beyond: Metrics-Based Evaluation of Scholarly Research* (Cambridge, MA: MIT Press, 2014); see also the collection of reprints by Blaise Cronin and Cassidy Sugimoto (eds.), *Scholarly Metrics under the Microscope: From Citation Analysis to Academic Auditing.* Medford, NJ: Information Today, Inc./ASIST, 2015.

6. Michel Zitt, "Book review of *Les dérives de l'évaluation de la recherche*" *Journal of the Association for Information Science and Technology* 66, no. 10 (October 2015): 2171–2176.

7. Ibid., p. 2175.

8. Pierre Vrignaud, "La mesure de la littératie dans PISA: La méthodologie est la réponse, mais quelle était la question?" *Education et formation*, no. 78 (November 2008): 69.

9. Some of these reflections have been published over the years in "Les systèmes d'évaluation de la recherche," *Documentaliste-Science de l'information*, 4 (November 2009): 34–35; "Du mauvais usage de faux indicateurs," *Revue d'histoire moderne et contemporaine* 5, no. 4bis (2008): 67–79 ; "Le classement de Shanghai n'est pas scientifique," *La Recherche*, May 2009: 46–50; "Marketing Can Corrupt Universities," *University Affairs* (January 2009); "Criteria for Evaluating Indicators," in *Bibliometrics and Beyond: Metrics-Based Evaluation of Scholarly Research*, Cronin and Sugimoto (eds.); "The Abuses of Research Evaluation," *University World News*, no. 306, February 7, 2014; and "How to Boost Your University up the Rankings," *University World News*, no. 329, July 18, 2014.

Chapter 1

1. Yuri V. Granosky, "Is It Possible to Measure Science? V. V. Nalimov's Research in Scientometrics," *Scientometrics* 52, no. 2 (2001): 127–150.

2. Alan Pritchard, "Statistical Bibliography or Bibliometrics?" *Journal of Documentation* 24 (1969): 348–349.

3. Virgil P. Diodato, *Dictionary of Bibliometrics* (New York: Haworth Press, 1994); Henk F. Moed, *Citation Analysis in Research Evaluation* (Dordrecht, the Netherlands: Springer, 2005), Nicola De Bellis, *Bibliometrics and Citation Analysis: From the Science Citation Index to Cybermetrics* (Lanham, MD: Scarecrow Press, 2009).

4. Alfred J. Lotka, "The Frequency Distribution of Scientific Productivity," *Journal of the Washington Academy of Sciences* 16, no. 12 (1926): 317–324.

5. Benoît Godin, "On the Origins of Bibliometrics," *Scientometrics* 68, no. 1 (2006): 109–133.

6. F. J. Cole and Nellie B. Eales, "The History of Comparative Anatomy. Part I: A Statistical Analysis of the Literature," *Science Progress* 11, no. 44 (1917): 578–596.

7. P. L. K. Gross and E. M. Gross, "College Libraries and Chemical Education," *Science* 66, no. 1713 (October 1927): 385–389.

8. Oden E. Shepard, "The Chemistry Student Still Needs a Reading Knowledge of German," *Journal of Chemical Education* 12, no. 10 (1935): 472–473.

9. Richard L. Barrett and Mildred A. Barrett, "Journals Most Cited by Chemists and Chemical Engineers," *Journal of Chemical Education,* 34, no. 1 (1957): 35–38.

10. Robert N. Broadus, "An Analysis of Literature Cited in the *American Sociological Review*," *American Sociological Review,* 17 (1952): 355–357.

11. Robert E. Burton and W. W. Kebler, "The 'Half-Life' of Some Scientific and Technical Literatures," *American Documentation,* 11, no.1 (1960): 18–22.

12. Norman T. Ball, "Review of 'The Royal Society Scientific Information Conference,' *Library Quarterly* 20, no. 1 (1950): 45.

13. William C. Adair, "Citation Indexes for Scientific Literature," *American Documentation* 6, no. 1 (1955): 31–32.

14. Eugene Garfield, "Citation Indexes for Science. A New Dimension in Documentation through Association of Ideas," *Science* 122, no. 5 (1955): 108–111.

15. For more details on the creation of ISI and SCI, see Paul Wouters, "The Citation Culture" (PhD dissertation, University of Amsterdam, 1999), accessed December 21, 2015, http://garfield.library.upenn.edu/wouters/wouters.pdf; see also Blaise Cronin

and Helen Barsky Atkins (eds.), *The Web of Knowledge. A Festschrift in Honor of Eugene Garfield* (Medford, NJ: ASIS Monograph Series, 2000).

16. Derek J. de Solla Price, "Quantitative Measures of the Development of Science," *Archives internationales d'histoire des sciences* 4, no. 14 (1951): 86–93. See also his two seminal books *Science since Babylon* (New Haven, CT: Yale University Press, 1961); and *Little Science, Big Science* (New York: Columbia University Press, 1963).

17. Kenneth O. May, "Quantitative Growth of the Mathematical Literature," *Science* 154, no. 3757 (1966): 1672–1673.

18. Derek J. de Solla Price, "Networks of Scientific Papers," *Science* 149, no. 3683 (1965): 510–515.

19. On the history of R&D statistics, see Benoît Godin, *Measurement and Statistics on Science and Technology* (London: Routledge, 2005).

20. OECD, "Proposed Standard Method for Surveys of Research and Development," in *The Measurement of Scientific and Technological Activities*, Directorate for Scientific Affairs, DAS/PD/62.47 (Paris: OECD, 1963).

21. Derek J. de Solla Price, "The Scientific Foundations of Science Policy," *Nature* 206, no. 4981 (1965): 233–238.

22. Francis Narin, *Evaluative Bibliometrics. The Use of Publication and Citation Analysis in the Evaluation of Scientific Activity* (Cherry Hill, NJ: Computer Horizons Inc., 1976); Francis Narin, Kimberly S. Hamilton, and Dominic Olivastro, "The Development of Science Indicators in the United States," in Blaise Cronin and Helen Barsky Atkins (eds.), *The Web of Knowledge*, 337–360.

23. Narin, Hamilton, and Olivastro, "The Development of Science Indicators in the United States," 352–353.

24. The main contributors were Derek de Solla Price, Eugene Garfield and his collaborator Henry Small, and sociologists Stephen and Jonathan R. Cole. Among the organizers, one finds the sociologist of science Robert K. Merton and the biologist Joshua Lederberg, who helped Garfield obtain research grants for his project at the end of the 1950s. See Yehuda Elkana, Joshua Lederberg, Robert K. Merton, Arnold Thackray, and Harriet Zuckerman (eds.), *Toward a Metric of Science. The Advent of Science Indicators* (New York: John Wiley & Sons, 1978).

25. Gerald Holton, "Can Science Be Measured?," in *Toward a Metric of Science. The Advent of Science Indicators*, Yehuda Elkana et al., eds., 39–68; Stephen Cole, Jonathan R. Cole, and Lorraine Dietrich, "Measuring the Cognitive State of Scientific Disciplines," ibid., 209–252 ; Eugene Garfield, Morton V. Malin, and Henry Small, "Citation Data as Science Indicators," ibid., 179–207.

26. T. D. Wilson, "The Nonsense of 'Knowledge Management,'" *Information Research* 8, no. 1 (2002), accessed December 21, 2015, http://InformationR.net/ir/8-1/paper144.html; Michael Power, "The Audit Society—Second Thoughts," *International Journal of Auditing* 4, no. 1 (2000): 111–119; Isabelle Bruno and Emmanuel Didier, *Benchmarking: L'État sous pression statistique* (Paris: La Découverte, 2013).

Chapter 2

1. Keith Pavitt, "Patent Statistics as Indicators of Innovative Activities: Possibilities and Problems," *Scientometrics* 7, no. 1–2 (1985): 77–99.

2. Francis Narin and Dominic Olivastro, "Linkage between Patents and Papers: An Interim EPO/US Comparison," *Scientometrics* 41, no. 1–2 (1998): 51–59.

3. Letter from Eugene Garfield to Harriet Zuckerman, August 18, 1971, cited by Paul Wouters, *The Citation Culture*, 102.

4. Eugene Garfield and Irving H. Sher, "The Use of Citation Data in Writing the History of Science," *American Documentation* 14, no. 3 (1963): 195–201; Eugene Garfield, "From the Science of Science to Scientometrics: Visualizing the History of Science with HistCite Software," *Journal of Informetrics* 3, no. 3 (2009): 173–179.

5. Henry Small, *Physics Citation Index, 1920–1929* (Philadelphia: ISI, 1981); Henry Small, "Recapturing Physics in the 1920s Through Citation Analysis," *Czechoslovak Journal of Physics*, 36, no. 1 (1986): 142–147.

6. See for details: http://wokinfo.com/products_tools/backfiles/coss, accessed December 21, 2015; and http://wokinfo.com/products_tools/backfiles/cos, accessed December 21, 2015.

7. David Edge, "Quantitative Measures of Communication in Science: A Critical Review," *History of Science* 17, no. 36, Pt. 2 (1979): 102–134.

8. Matthew L. Wallace, Vincent Larivière, and Yves Gingras, "Modeling a Century of Citation Distributions," *Journal of Informetrics* 3, no. 4 (2009): 296–303.

9. Daniele Fanelli and Vincent Larivière, "Are Scientists Really Publishing More?" *Proceedings of the 15th International Conference of the International Society for Scientometrics and Informetrics* (2015): 652–653.

10. Eugene Garfield and Irving H. Sher, "New Factors in the Evaluation of Scientific Literature through Citation Indexing," *American Documentation* 14, no. 3 (1963): 195–201.

11. Vincent Larivière, Benoît Macaluso, Éric Archambault, and Yves Gingras, "Which Scientific Elites? On the Concentration of Research Funds, Publications, and Citations," *Research Evaluation* 19, no. 1 (2010): 45–53.

12. Robert K. Merton, *The Sociology of Science* (Chicago: University of Chicago Press, 1973), 449–459; Daniel Rigney, *The Matthew Effect. How Advantage Begets Further Advantage* (New York: Columbia University Press, 2010).

13. Alan E. Bayer and John K. Folger, "Some Correlates of a Citation Measure of Productivity in Science," *Sociology of Education* 39 (1966): 381–390.

14. Eugene Garfield and Irving H. Sher, "New Tools for Improving and Evaluating the Effectiveness of Research," in *Research Program Effectiveness, Proceedings of the Conference Sponsored by the Office of Naval Research, Washington, D.C., July 27–29, 1965*, M. C. Yovits, D. M. Gilford, R. H. Wilcox, E. Staveley, and H. D. Lemer, eds. (New York: Gordon and Breach, 1966), 135–146, accessed December 21, 2015, http://www.garfield.library.upenn.edu/papers/onrpaper.html.

15. Jonathan R. Cole and Stephen Cole, *Social Stratification in Science* (Chicago: University of Chicago Press, 1973).

16. Yu Liu, Weijia Li, Zhen Huang, and Qiang Fang, "A Fast Method Based on Multiple Clustering for Name Disambiguation in Bibliographic Citations," *Journal of the Association for Information Science and Technology*, 66, no. 3 (2015): 634–644; Ciriaco Andrea D'Angelo, Cristiano Giuffrida, and Giovanni Abramo, "A Heuristic Approach to Author Name Disambiguation in Bibliometrics Databases for Large-Scale Research Assessments," *Journal of the American Society for Information Science and Technology*, 62, no. 2 (2011): 257–269.

17. Perry W. Wilson and Edwin B. Fred, "The Growth Curve of a Scientific Literature," *Scientific Monthly* 41 (1935): 240–250.

18. Jack H. Westbrook, "Identifying Significant Research," *Science* 132, no. 3435 (1960): 1229–1234; J. C. Fisher, "Basic Research in Industry. A Count of Scientific Publications Suggests the Extent of U.S. Industry's Effort in Basic Research," *Science* 129, no. 3364 (1959): 1653–1657.

19. G. Nigel Gilbert, "Measuring the Growth of Science. A Review of Indicators of Scientific Growth," *Scientometrics* 1, no. 1 (1978): 9–34.

20. Olessia Kirchik, Yves Gingras, and Vincent Larivière, "Changes in Publication Languages and Citation Practices and Their Effect on the Scientific Impact of Russian Science (1993–2010)," *Journal of the American Society for Information Science and Technology* 63, no. 7 (2012): 1411–1419.

21. See, for example, A. Schubert, W. Glänzel, and T. Braun, "Scientometric Datafiles. A Comprehensive Set of Indicators on 2649 Journals and 96 Countries in All Major Science Fields and Subfields, 1981–1985," *Scientometrics* 16, no. 1–6 (1989): 3–478.

22. Francis Narin, "Patent Bibliometrics," *Scientometrics* 30, no. 1 (1994): 147–155.

23. P. W. Hart and J. T. Sommerfeld, "Relationship between Growth in Gross Domestic Product (GDP) and Growth in the Chemical Engineering Literature in Five Different Countries," *Scientometrics* 42, no. 3 (1998): 299–311.

24. Vincent Larivière, Éric Archambault, Yves Gingras, and Etienne Vignola-Gagné, "The Place of Serials in Referencing Practices: Comparing Natural Sciences and Engineering with Social Sciences and Humanities," *Journal of the American Society for Information Science and Technology* 57, no. 8 (2006): 997–1004.

25. Elisabeth S. Clemens, Walter W. Powell, Kris McIlwaine, and Dina Okamoto, "Careers in Print: Books, Journals, and Scholarly Reputations," *American Journal of Sociology* 101, no. 2 (1995): 433–494.

26. Yves Gingras, "L'évolution des collaborations scientifiques entre le Québec, le Canada et l'union européenne (1980–2009)," *Globe. Revue internationale d'études québécoises* 14, no. 2 (2011): 185–197.

27. Vincent Larivière and Yves Gingras, "Measuring Interdisciplinarity," in *Beyond Bibliometrics: Harnessing Multidimensional Indicators of Scholarly Impact*, Blaise Cronin and Cassidy R. Sugimoto, eds. (Cambridge, MA: MIT Press, 2014), 187–200.

28. Yves Gingras, "The Transformation of Physics from 1900 to 1945," *Physics in Perspective* 12, no. 3 (2010): 248–265.

29. S. Phineas Upham and Henry Small, "Emerging Research Fronts in Science and Technology: Patterns of New Knowledge Development," *Scientometrics* 83, no. 1 (2010): 15–38; Dangzhi Zhao and Andrew Strotmann, "Can Citation Analysis of Web Publications Better Detect Research Fronts?" *Journal of the American Society for Information Science and Technology* 58, no. 9 (2007): 1285–1302.

30. Michael M. Kessler, "Bibliographic Coupling between Scientific Papers," *American Documentation* 14, no. 1 (1963): 10–25.

31. Henry Small, "Co-Citation in Scientific Literature: A New Measure of Relationship between Two Documents," *Journal of the American Society for Information Science* 24, no. 4 (1973): 265–269.

32. Matthew L. Wallace, Yves Gingras, and Russell Duhon, "A New Approach for Detecting Scientific Specialties from Raw Cocitation Networks," *Journal of the American Society for Information Science and Technology* 60, no. 2 (2009): 240–246.

33. Kevin W. Boyack, Richard Klavans, and Katy Börner, "Mapping the Backbone of Science," *Scientometrics* 64, no. 3 (2005): 351–374; Katy Börner, Richard Klavans, Michael Patek, Angela Zoss, Joseph R. Biberstine, Robert Light, Vincent Larivière, and Kevin W. Boyack, Design and Update of a Classification System: The UCSD Map of Science. *PLoS ONE* 7, no. 7 (2012): e39464.

34. Jean Piaget, "Le système et la classification des sciences," in *Logique et connaissance scientifique*, Jean Piaget, ed. (Paris: Gallimard, 1967), 1151–1224.

35. See the many representations in Katy Börner, *Atlas of Science. Visualizing What We Know* (Cambridge, MA: MIT Press, 2010); see also: scimaps.org/atlas/maps, accessed December 21, 2015.

36. Council of Canadian Academies, *Informing Research Choices: Indicators and Judgment* (Ottawa: Council of Canadian Academies, 2012).

37. Here, the age of the cited literature is measured as the difference between the year of publication and the year of the cited reference. Vincent Larivière, Éric Archambault, and Yves Gingras, "Long-Term Variations in the Aging of Scientific Literature: From Exponential Growth to Steady-State Science (1900–2004)," *Journal of the American Society for Information Science and Technology* 59 (2008): 288–296.

38. Wallace, Larivière, and Gingras, "Modeling a Century of Citation Distributions."

39. Vincent Larivière, Éric Archambault, Yves Gingras, and Matthew L. Wallace, "The Fall of Uncitedness," in *Book of Abstracts of the 10th International Conference on Science and Technology Indicators* (2008): 279–282.

40. C. King, "Cold Fusion, Yes or No," *Science Watch* 1, no. 3 (1990): 7–8; see also *New Scientist*, no. 1713, April 21, 1990, "In Brief: Citations Track the Fate of Cold Fusion."

41. Michael J. Moravcsik and Poovanalingam Murugesan, "Some Results on the Function and Quality of Citations," *Social Studies of Science* 5, no. 1 (February 1975): 86–92.

42. Anthony F. J. van Raan, "Sleeping Beauty in Science," *Scientometrics* 59, no. 3 (2004): 461–466.

43. Yves Gingras, "La carrière des publications d'Ettore Majorana. Une étude bibliométrique," *Revue de synthèse* 134, no. 1 (2013): 75–87.

44. Peter A. Lawrence, "The Mismeasurement of Science," *Current Biology* 17, no. 15 (2007): R584–R585.

45. Francesco Becattini, Arnab Chatterjee, Santo Fortunato, Marija Mitrović, Raj Kumar Pan, and Pietro Della Briotta Parolo, "The Nobel Prize Delay," arXiv: 1405.7136v1 [physics.soc-ph], May 28, 2014.

46. Yves Gingras, "Revisiting the 'Quiet Debut' of the Double Helix: A Bibliometric and Methodological Note on the 'Impact' of Scientific Publications," *Journal of the History of Biology* 43, no. 1 (2010): 159–181.

47. Yves Gingras, "The Collective Construction of Scientific Memory: The Einstein-Poincaré Connection and Its Discontents, 1905–2005," *History of Science* 46, no. 1 (March 2008): 75–114; Gingras, "The Transformation of Physics from 1900 to 1945."

48. Eugene Garfield, "Random Thoughts on Citationology. Its Theory and Practice," *Scientometrics* 43, no. 1 (1998): 69–76.

49. Eugene Garfield, "'Science Citation Index'. A New Dimension in Indexing," *Science*, 144, no. 3619 (May 1964): 649–654.

50. Norman Kaplan, "The Norms of Citation Behavior: Prolegomena to the Footnote," *American Documentation* 16, no. 3 (1965): 179–184.

51. Warren O. Hagstrom, *The Scientific Community* (New York: Basic Books, 1965).

52. Derek de Solla Price, *Little Science, Big Science* (New York: Columbia University Press, 1963), 65.

53. Charles Bazerman, *Shaping Written Knowledge* (Madison: University of Wisconsin Press, 1988).

54. James E. McClellan, *Specialist Control. The Publications Committee of the Académie Royale des Sciences (Paris), 1700–1793* (Philadelphia: American Philosophical Society, 2003), 33.

55. For a survey, see Loet Leydesdorff, "Theories of Citation?" *Scientometrics* 43, no. 1 (1998): 5–25; Julian Warner, "A Critical Review of the Application of Citation Studies to the Research Assessment Exercises," *Journal of Information Science*, 26, no. 6 (2000): 453–460.

56. Blaise Cronin, *The Citation Process. The Role and Significance of Citations in Scientific Communication* (London: Taylor Graham, 1984). For a recent review of citations, see Jeppe Nicolaisen, "Citation Analysis," *Annual Review of Information Science and Technology* 41, no. 1 (2007): 609–641.

57. Gingras, "The Collective Construction of Scientific Memory."

58. G. Nigel Gilbert, "Referencing as Persuasion," *Social Studies of Science* 7, no. 1 (1977): 113–122.

59. Joseph Bensman, "The Aesthetics and Politics of Footnoting," *Politics, Culture, and Society* 1, no. 3 (1988): 443–470; paradoxically, this long essay contains no references or data, but it does speculate on strategic citations and the inflation of self-citations.

60. Vincent Larivière, Alesia Zuccala, and Éric Archambault, "The Declining Scientific Impact of Theses: Implications for Electronic Thesis and Dissertation Repositories and Graduate Studies," *Scientometrics* 74, no. 1 (2008): 109–121; see also Matthew L. Wallace, Vincent Larivière, and Yves Gingras, "A Small World of Citations? The Influence of Collaboration Networks on Citation Practices," *PLoS ONE* 7, no. 3 (2012), e33339, doi: 10.1371/journal.pone.0033339.

61. Susan Bonzi and Herbert W. Snyder, "Motivations for Citation: A Comparison of Self Citations and Citations to Others," *Scientometrics* 21, no. 2 (1991): 245–254 ;

see also Béatrice Milard, "The Social Circles behind Scientific References: Relationships between Citing and Cited Authors in Chemistry Publications," *Journal of the Association for Information Science and Technology* 65, no. 12 (2014): 2459–2468; Martin G Erikson and Peter Erlandson, "A Taxonomy of Motives to Cite," *Social Studies of Science* 44, no. 4 (2014): 625–637.

Chapter 3

1. European Science Foundation (ESF), *ESF Survey Analysis Report on Peer Review Practices*, ESF, March 2011, accessed December 21, 2015, www.esf.org/fileadmin/Public_documents/Publications/pr_guide_survey.pdf.

2. Marie Boas Hall, *Henry Oldenburg: Shaping the Royal Society* (Oxford, UK: Oxford University Press, 2002), 84. The *Journal des savants*, published by Denis de Sallo, began in January 1665, but was censured by the King of France (Louis XIV) three months later. It soon reappeared but its content remained very heterogeneous and covered all the activities of the republic of letters. It was, thus, more a literary gazette than a peer-reviewed scientific journal like the *Proceedings*.

3. Ibid., 167–170.

4. Arthur J. Meadows, *Communication in Science* (London: Butterworths, 1974), 66–90.

5. Lewis Pyenson, "Physical Sense in Relativity: Max Planck Edits the *Annalen der Physik*, 1906–1918," *Annalen der Physik* 17, no. 2–3 (2008): 176–189.

6. For more details, see Daniel Kennefick, "Einstein versus the *Physical Review*," *Physics Today* 58, no. 9 (2005): 43–48.

7. Yves Gingras, *Physics and the Rise of Scientific Research in Canada* (Montreal: McGill–Queen's University Press, 1991).

8. James M. England, *A Patron for Pure Science: The National Science Foundation's Formative Years, 1945–57* (Washington DC: NSF, 1982); Roger L. Geiger, *To Advance Knowledge: The Growth of American Research Universities, 1900–1940* (New York: Oxford University Press, 1986); Gerald Jonas, *The Circuit Riders: Rockefeller Money and the Rise of Modern Science* (New York: W.W. Norton, 1989).

9. Stephen Cole, Jonathan R. Cole, and Gary A. Simon, "Chance and Consensus in Peer Review," *Science* 214, no. 4523 (1981): 881–886.

10. For a detailed study on judgment criteria, see Michèle Lamont, *How Professors Think: Inside the Curious World of Academic Judgment* (Cambridge, MA: Harvard University Press, 2009).

11. For an analysis of the relation between numbers and objectivity, see Theodore M. Porter, *Trust in Numbers: The Pursuit of Objectivity in Science and Public Life* (Princeton, NJ: Princeton University Press, 1996).

12. Thane Gustafson, "The Controversy over Peer Review," *Science* 190, no. 4219 (December 1975): 1060–1066. Recent bibliometric studies still confirm the general validity of peer review; see Jeffrey Mervis, "NIH's Peer Review Stands Up to Scrutiny," *Science*, 348, no. 6233 (2015), 384.

13. R. N. Kostoff, "Performance Measures for Government-Sponsored Research: Overview and Background," *Scientometrics* 36, no. 3 (1996): 281–292; for a recent and complete survey of the literature, see Paul Wouters, Mike Thelwall, Kayvan Kousha, Ludo Waltman, Sarah de Rijcke, Alex Rushforth, and Thomas Franssen, *The Metric Tide: Literature Review (Supplementary Report I to the Independent Review of the Role of Metrics in Research Assessment and Management)* (HEFCE, 2015).

14. See, for example, David Crouch, John Irvine, and Ben R. Martin, "Bibliometric Analysis for Science Policy: An Evaluation of the United Kingdom's Research Performance in Ocean Currents and Protein Crystallography," *Scientometrics* 9, no. 5–6 (1986): 239–267; K. C. Garg and M. K. D. Rao, "Bibliometric Analysis of Scientific Productivity: A Case Study of an Indian Physics Laboratory," *Scientometrics* 13, no. 5 (1988): 261–269.

15. It would be easy to give numerous examples, but one should suffice. In a paper published in 2015 in a journal generally considered as "prestigious," the *Proceedings of the National Academy of Science*, the authors studied negative citations and (incorrectly) affirmed that "we know little about the different ways in which a study can be cited"; see Christian Catalini, Nicola Lacetera, and Alexander Oetti, "The Incidence and Role of Negative Citation in Science," *Proceedings of the National Academy of Science* 112, no. 45 (2015): 13823–13826. Among the 28 references in that paper, none were to any of the standard journals in bibliometrics, where the authors would have found a great many papers on the topic of negative citations and motivations for citing. For a recent review of citations, see Jeppe Nicolaisen, "Citation Analysis," in Blaise Cronin (ed.), *Annual Review of Information Science and Technology* 41 (2007), 609–641.

16. For an analysis of the hiring process in different countries, see Christine Musselin, *Le Marché des universitaires* (Paris: Presses de Sciences Po, 2006).

17. Eugene Garfield, "Citation Indexes in Sociological and Historical Research," *American Documentation* 14, no. 4, 1963, 289–291.

18. Eugene Garfield, "Citation Indexing for Studying Science," *Nature* 227 (1970): 669–671.

19. Yves Gingras and Matthew L. Wallace, "Why It Has Become More Difficult to Predict Nobel Prize Winners: A Bibliometric Analysis of Nominees and Winners of

the Chemistry and Physics Prizes (1901–2007)," *Scientometrics* 82, no. 2 (February 2010): 401–412.

20. Garfield, "Citation Indexing for Studying Science," 671.

21. Janet B. Bavelas, "The Social Psychology of Citations," *Canadian Psychological Review* 19, no. 2 (1978): 158–163.

22. Porter, *Trust in Numbers*.

23. Nicholas Wade, "Citation Analysis: A New Tool for Science Administrators," *Science* 188, no. 4187 (1975): 429–432.

24. Jorge E. Hirsch, "An Index to Quantify an Individual's Scientific Research Output," *Proceedings of the National Academy of Sciences* 102, no. 46 (2005): 16569–16572.

25. Thed N. van Leeuwen, "Testing the Validity of the Hirsch-Index for Research Assessment Purposes," *Research Evaluation* 17, no. 2 (2008): 157–160.

26. Ludo Waltman and Nees Jan van Eck, "The Inconsistency of the H-Index," ArXiv:1108.3901v1 (August 19, 2011).

27. The question of the best normalization is a very technical one that is debated by experts in bibliometrics; for a discussion, see, for example, Michel Zitt, Suzy Ramana-Rahary, and Elise Bassecoulard, "Relativity of Citation Performance and Excellence Measures: From Cross-Field to Cross-Scale Effects of Field-Normalisation," *Scientometrics* 63, no. 2 (2005): 373–401; Loet Leydesdorff, Filippo Radicchi, Lutz Bornmann, Claudio Castellano, and Wouter de Nooy, "Field-Normalized Impact Factors: A Comparison of Rescaling versus Fractionally Counted Ifs," *Journal of the American Society for Information Science and Technology* 64, no 11 (2013): 2299–2309; Lutz Bornmann, Loet Leydesdorff, and Jian Wang, "Which Percentile-Based Approach Should Be Preferred for Calculating Normalized Citation Impact Values? An Empirical Comparison of Five Approaches Including a Newly Developed One (P100)," *Journal of Informetrics* 7, no 4 (2013), 933 944.

28. Unfortunately, the h-index has also given rise to a speculative "bubble" among experts in bibliometrics. Many papers forget to question its validity before using it in different ways, often trying to correct its obvious defects by dividing or multiplying it with other variables like age. For an analysis of this bubble, see Ronald Rousseau, Carlos García-Zorita, and Elias Sanz-Casado, "The H-Bubble," *Journal of Informetrics* 7, no. 2 (2013): 294–300.

29. Sophie L. Rovner, "The Import of Impact: New Types of Journal Metrics Grow More Influential in the Scientific Community," *C&EN Chemical and Engineering News* 86, no. 21 (2008): 39–42.

30. Robert Adler, John Ewing, and Peter Taylor, "'Citation Statistics,' A Report from the International Mathematical Union (IMU) in Cooperation with the International

Council of Industrial and Applied Mathematics (ICIAM) and the Institute of Mathematical Statistics (IMS)," *Statistical Science* 24 (2009): 1–14.

31. For a history of this journal indicator, see Éric Archambault and Vincent Larivière, "History of Journal Impact Factor: Contingencies and Consequences," *Scientometrics* 79, no. 3 (2009): 639–653, and Stephen J. Bensman, "Garfield and the Impact Factor," *Annual Review of Information Science and Technology* 41, no. 1 (2007): 93–155.

32. Wolfgang Glänzel and Henk F. Moed, "Journal Impact Measures in Bibliometric Research," *Scientometrics* 53, no. 2 (2002): 171–193.

33. Allen W. Wilhite and Eric A. Fong, "Coercive Citation in Academic Publishing," *Science* 335, no. 3 (February 2012): 542–543.

34. Richard Smith, "Journal Accused of Manipulating Impact Factor," *British Medical Journal* 314, no. 7079 (1997): 461; Frank-Thorsten Krell, "Should Editors Influence Journal Impact Factors?" *Library Publishing* 23, no. 1 (2010): 59–62.

35. James Testa, "Playing the System Puts Self-Citation's Impact Under Review," *Nature* 455, no. 7214 (2008): 729.

36. Paul Jump, "Journal Citation Cartels on the Rise," *Times Higher Education*, June 21, 2013, accessed December 21, 2015, http://www.timeshighereducation.co.uk/news/journal-citation-cartels-on-the-rise/2005009.article.

37. On the sociological basis of scientific deviance and fraud, see Robert K. Merton, *The Sociology of Science* (Chicago: University of Chicago Press, 1973), 309–321.

38. Richard Van Noorden, "Brazilian Citation Scheme Outed: Thomson Reuters Suspends Journals from Its Rankings for 'Citation Stacking,'" *Nature* 500, no. 7460 (2013): 510–511.

39. For a case involving a journal of criminology, see Thomas Baker, "An Evaluation of Journal Impact Factors: A Case Study of the Top Three Journals Ranked in Criminology and Penology," *The Criminologist* 40, no. 5 (2015): 5–13.

40. Editorial, "Not so Deep Impact," *Nature* 545, no. 7045 (2005): 1003–1004.

41. Per O. Seglen, "Why the Impact Factor of Journals Should Not Be Used for Evaluating Research," *British Medical Journal* 314, no. 7079 (1997): 498–502; Henk F. Moed, "The Future of Research Evaluation Rests with an Intelligent Combination of Advanced Metrics and Transparent Peer Review," *Science and Public Policy* 34, no 8 (2007): 575–583.

42. See for example, Editorial, "China's Medical Research Integrity Questioned," *The Lancet*, 385, no. 9976 (April 11, 2015): 1365.

43. Ichiko Fuyuno and David Cyranoski, "Cash for Papers: Putting a Premium on Publication," *Nature* 441, no. 7095 (June 15, 2006): 792; see also, in the same issue, Editorial, "Cash-per-Publication," 786.

44. Bruce Alberts, "Impact Factor Distortions," *Science* 340, no. 6134 (May 17, 2013): 787.

45. American Society for Cell Biology, "San Francisco Declaration on Research Assessment," accessed December 21, 2015, http://am.ascb.org/dora.

46. Nicolas Gallois, "Les conséquences des nouveaux critères d'évaluation des chercheurs en science économique," *L'économie politique* 59 (2013): 98–112. It is worth noting that Eugene Garfield himself "deplored the quotation of impact factors to three decimal places. ISI uses three decimal places to reduce the number of journals with the identical impact rank. It matters very little whether the impact of JAMA is quoted as 21.5 rather than 21.455"; see Eugene Garfield, "The Agony and the Ecstasy—The History and Meaning of the Journal Impact Factor," International Congress on Peer Review and Biomedical Publication Chicago, September 16, 2005, p. 5, http://garfield.library.upenn.edu/papers/jifchicago2005.pdf.

47. For a list of such perverse effects, see Arturo Casadevall and Ferric C. Fang, "Causes for the Persistence of Impact Factor Mania," *mBio* 5, no. 2 (2014): 1–5; for a sociological analysis of law school rankings, see W. N. Espeland and M. Sauder, "Rankings and Reactivity: How Public Measure Recreates Social Worlds," *American Journal of Sociology* 113, no.1 (2007): 1–40.

48. Richard van Noorden, "Nature Owner Merges with Publishing Giant," *Nature,* January 15, 2015, http://www.nature.com/news/nature-owner-merges-with -publishing-giant-1.16731.

49. http://www.natureindex.com/faq#introduction2, accessed December 28, 2015.

50. For a comparison of existing rankings and their various indicators, see http://www.universityrankings.ch, accessed December 21, 2015. For a critical analysis, see Malcolm Gladwell, "The Order of Things. What College Rankings Really Tell Us," *The New Yorker*, February 14–21, 2011, pp. 68–75, and Alia Wong, "College-Ranking World," *The Atlantic,* November 9, 2015, accessed December 21, 2015, http://www .theatlantic.com/education/archive/2015/11/a-college-rankings-world/414759/.

51. Joël Bourdin, *Rapport d'information fait au nom de la délégation du Sénat pour la Planification sur le défi des classements dans l'enseignement supérieur.* Appendix to the minutes of the July 2, 2008 meeting, p. 53, accessed December 21, 2015, http:// www.senat.fr/rap/r07-442/r07-4421.pdf.

52. Paris Tech Mines, *International Professional Ranking of Higher Education Institutions*, 2011, p. 1, accessed December 21, 2015, http://www.mines-paristech.fr/ Donnees/data03/334-10.-Classements.pdf.

53. For details, see www.rae.ac.uk, accessed December 21, 2015.

54. For details, see http://www.ref.ac.uk, accessed December 21, 2015.

55. Higher Education Funding Council for England (HEFCE), *The Metric Tide: Correlation Analysis of REF2014 Scores and Metrics (Supplementary Report II to the Independent Review of the Role of Metrics in Research Assessment and Management)*, 2015, HEFCE. DOI: 10.13140/RG.2.1.3362.4162.

56. "Accountability Review Puts the Cost of REF 2014 at Almost £250 Million," *Times Higher Education*, July 13, 2015, accessed December 21, 2015, https://www.timeshighereducation.com/news/ref-2014-cost-250-million.

57. http://www.ref.ac.uk, accessed December 21, 2015.

58. Linda Butler, "Explaining Australia's Increased Share of ISI Publications: The Effects of a Funding Formula Based on Publication Counts," *Research Policy* 31, no.1 (2003): 143–155; see also, by the same author, "Assessing University Research: A Plea for a Balanced Approach," *Science and Public Policy* 34, no. 8 (2007): 565–574; for information about the Flanders situation, see Koenraad Debackere and Wolfgang Glänzel, "Using a Bibliometric Approach to Support Research Policy Making: The Case of the Flemish BOF-Key," *Scientometrics* 59, no. 2 (2004): 253–276.

59. Karen Stroobants, Simon Godecharle, and Sofie Brouwers, "Flanders Overrates Impact Factors," *Nature* 500, no. 7460 (August 2013): 29.

60. Council of Canadian Academies, *Informing Research Choices*, 120.

61. Linda Butler, "Modifying Publication Practices in Response to Funding Formulas," *Research Evaluation* 12, no. 1 (2003): 39–46; Henk F. Moed, "UK Research Assessment Exercises: Informed Judgments on Research Quality or Quantity?" *Scientometrics* 74, no. 1 (2008): 153–161; Valerie Bence and Charles Oppenheim, "The Role of Academic Journal Publications in the UK Research Assessment Exercise," *Learned Publishing* 17, no. 1 (2004): 53–68.

62. Maya Beauvallet, *Les Stratégies absurdes. Comment faire pire en croyant faire mieux* (Paris: Seuil, 2009), 67.

63. Council of Canadian Academies, *Informing Research Choices*, xiii.

64. HEFCE (2015), *The Metric Tide*, viii–x.

65. A brief full-text search in the *Journal of Economic Literature* shows that the term "United States" generates 420 documents, while "France" produces only 165 and "monetary union" only 11, which suggests that all economic objects are not born equal in the so-called top journals.

66. Wayne Simpson and J.C. Herbert Emery, "Canadian Economics in Decline: Implications for Canada's Economics Journals," *Canadian Public Policy* 38, no. 4 (2012): 445–470.

67. See "Classement européen des revues," accessed December 21, 2015, http://www.cnrs.fr/inshs/recherche/classement-europeen-revues.htm; Françoise Briatte, "Comparaison inter-classement des revues en sociologie-démographie et en science politique," *Bulletin de méthodologie sociologique* 100, no. 1 (2008): 51–60.

68. Yves Gingras and Sébastien Mosbah-Natanson, "La question de la traduction en sciences sociales: Les revues françaises entre visibilité internationale et ancrage national," *Archives européennes de sociologie* 51, no. 2 (2010): 305–321.

69. This brief analysis has been done using the function "Analyze results" in the Thomson Reuters WoS database.

70. "Journals under Threat: A Joint Response from History of Science, Technology, and Medicine Editors," Editorial published in many journals; see, for example, *Medical History* 53, no. 1 (2009): 1–4, or *Social Studies of Science* 39, no. 1 (2009): 6–9.

71. Pierre Bourdieu, *On Television* (New York: New Press, 1998), 95.

72. See: http://theconversation.com/journal-rankings-ditched-the-experts-respond-1598, accessed December 21, 2015; see also Jerome K. Vanclay, "An Evaluation of the Australian Research Council's Journal Ranking," *Journal of Informetrics* 5, no. 2 (2011): 265–274.

73. For details, see Anne Saada, "L'évaluation et le classement des revues de sciences humaines par l'Agence de l'évaluation de la recherche et de l'enseignement supérieur (AERES)," *Connexions* 93 (2010): 199–204; David Pontille and Didier Torny, "Rendre publique l'évaluation des SHS: Les controverses sur les listes de revues de l'AERES," *Quaderni* 77, no. 1 (2012): 11–24.

Chapter 4

1. J. Wilsdon et al., *The Metric Tide: Report of the Independent Review of the Role of Metrics in Research Assessment and Management*, HEFCE 2015, DOI: 10.13140/RG.2.1.4929.1363.

2. For a systematic analysis of the validity of a large number of bibliometric indicators, see Council of Canadian Academies, *Informing Research Choices,* Appendix C, accessed December 21, 2015. http://www.scienceadvice.ca/uploads/eng/assessments%20and%20publications%20and%20news%20releases/science%20performance/scienceperformance_en_appendixbc_web.pdf.

3. Jason Priem, "Altmetrics," in *Beyond Bibliometrics: Harnessing Multidimensional Indicators for Scholarly Impact,* Blaise Cronin and Cassidy R. Sugimoto, eds. (Cambridge, MA: MIT Press, 2014), 263–287.

4. Emilio López-Cózar, Nicolás Robinson-García, and Daniel Torres-Salinas, "Manipulating Google Scholar Citations and Google Scholar Metrics: Simple, Easy, and Tempting," https://arxiv.org/ftp/arxiv/papers/1212/1212.0638.pdf, 2013.

5. See http://bibliometrie.wordpress.com/2011/05/12/ike-antkare-i-dont-care, accessed December 21, 2015.

6. For more details, see http://plumanalytics.com and http://www.academicanalytics .com, accessed March 22, 2016.

7. Colleen Flaherty, "Refusing to Be Evaluated by a Formula," *Inside Higher Ed*, December 11, 2015, https://www.insidehighered.com/news/2015/12/11/rutgers -professors-object-contract-academic-analytics, accessed March 22, 2016.

8. Philippe Mongeon and Adèle Paul-Hus, "The Journal Coverage of Web of Science and Scopus: A Comparative Analysis," *Scientometrics*, October 19, 2015, DOI: 10.1007/s11192-015-1765-5; see also http://hlwiki.slais.ubc.ca/index.php/Scopus _vs._Web_of_Science? accessed December 21, 2015.

9. See, for example, Anne-Marie Kermarrec et al., "Que mesurent les indicateurs bibliométriques?" Document d'analyze de la commission d'évaluation de l'INRIA, 2007, accessed December 21, 2015, http://www.ias.u-psud.fr/pperso/fbaudin/docs/ RappINRIA.pdf.

10. Éric Archambault, David Campbell, Yves Gingras, and Vincent Larivière, "Comparing Bibliometric Statistics Obtained from the Web of Science and Scopus," *Journal of the American Society for Information Science and Technology* 60, no. 7 (2009): 1320–1326; for an update of these data, see Mongeon and Paul-Hus, "The Journal Coverage of Web of Science and Scopus."

11. J. Priem, D. Taraborelli, P. Groth, and C. Neylon, "Altmetrics: A Manifesto," October 26, 2010, http://altmetrics.org/manifesto, accessed December 21, 2015.

12. For a recent survey of altmetrics, see Samanta Work, Stefanie Haustein, Timothy D. Bowman, and Vincent Larivière, *Social Media in Scholarly Communication: A Review of the Literature and Empirical Analysis of Twitter Use by SSHRC Doctoral Award Recipients*. Study commissioned by the Social Sciences and Humanities Research Council (2015), accessed December 21, 2015, http://crctcs.openum.ca/files/sites/60/2015/12/ SSHRC_SocialMediainScholarlyCommunication.pdf.

13. Stefanie Haustein et al., "Tweeting Biomedicine: An Analysis of Tweets and Citations in the Biomedical Literature," *Journal of the Association for Information Science and Technology* 65, no. 4 (2014): 656–669.

14. Benjamin Rey, "Your Tweet Half-Life Is 1 Billion Times Shorter than Carbon-14s," http://www.wiselytics.com/blog/tweet-isbillion-time-shorter-than-carbon14/, accessed December 21, 2015.

15. Stéphane Mercure, Frédéric Bertrand, Éric Archambault, and Yves Gingras, "Impacts socioéconomiques de la recherche financée par le gouvernement du Québec, via les Fonds subventionnaires québécois. Études de cas," Rapport présenté au Ministère du Développement économique, de l'Innovation et de l'Exportation du Québec, 2007.

16. James Pringle, "Trends in the Use of ISI Citation Databases for Evaluation," *Learned Publishing* 21, no. 2 (2008): 85–91.

17. Johan Bollen, Herbert Van de Sompel, Aric Hagberg, and Ryan Chute, "A Principal Component Analysis of 39 Scientific Impact Measures," *PLoS ONE* 4, no. 6 (2009) e6022, doi:10.1371/journal.pone.0006022.

18. Jamil Salmi and Alenoush Saroyan, "League Tables as Policy Instruments: Uses and Misuses," *Higher Education Management and Policy* 19, no.2 (2007): 31–68; Ellen Hazelkorn, "The Impact of League Tables and Ranking Systems in Higher Education Decision Making," *Higher Education Management and Policy* 19, no. 2 (2007): 87–110.

19. *IREG Ranking Audit Manual*, Brussels, IREG, 2011, pp. 21–22, accessed December 21, 2015, http://www.iregobservatory.org/pdf/ranking_audith_audit.pdf. Confronted with the multiplication of evaluation schemes, a group of expert colleagues in bibliometrics has also suggested a series of ten principles to guide evaluation, but they take for granted that the chosen indicators are valid, without providing definite criteria that would prove it. Before using multiple indicators, one must first assess their validity, for two wrongs does not make a right; see Diana Hicks et al., "Bibliometrics: The Leiden Manifesto for Research Metrics," *Nature* 520, no. 7548 (April 2015): 429–431.

20. Council of Canadian Academies, *Informing Research Choices: Indicators and Judgment* (Ottawa: Council of Canadian Academies, 2012), 64.

21. Pascal Pansu, Nicole Dubois, and Jean-Léon Beauvois, *Dis-moi qui te cite, et je te dirai ce que tu vaux. Que mesure vraiment la bibliométrie?* (Grenoble: Presses universitaires de Grenoble, 2013), 93.

22. Paul F. Lazarsfeld, "Evidence and Inference in Social Research," *Daedalus* 87, no. 4 (1958): 99–130.

23. Jonathan R. Cole and Stephen Cole, *Social Stratification in Science* (Chicago: University of Chicago Press, 1973).

24. Merton, *The Sociology of Science* (Chicago: University of Chicago Press, 1973).

25. Larivière et al., "The Place of Serials in Referencing Practices"; Éric Archambault et al., "Benchmarking Scientific Output in the Social Sciences and Humanities: The Limits of Existing Databases," *Scientometrics* 68, no. 3 (2006): 329–342.

26. Ranking Web of Universities, 2012, Methodology, paragraph 22, accessed December 21, 2015, http://www.webometrics.info/en/Methodology.

27. It is absurd, for instance, to state that "education should be tied to the extremely volatile labour market," since education operates on time scales that are incompatible with those of the job market (cited in "Les cahiers de la compétitivité," *Le Monde*, May 21, 2008, p. 1). This problem highlights the importance of having basic training that transcends this volatility.

28. Jeremiah P. Ostriker, Charlotte V. Kuh, and James A. Voytuk, eds., Committee to Assess Research-Doctorate Programs; National Research Council, *A Data-Based Assessment of Research-Doctorate Programs in the United States* (Washington: National Academy Press, 2011), accessible at http://www.nap.edu/rdp.

29. Adding up many indicators with different measures is what makes the indicator heterogeneous. In the case of the price index, for example, we add different objects (eggs, meat, etc.) but the unit is the price, which is homogeneous. It would not make sense to sum up the number of units of the different objects themselves because they are heterogeneous. So a composite index can be homogeneous, but then one must make sure that the weight given to each component is not arbitrarily chosen.

30. See, for example, the methodology of the world university ranking of the *Times Higher Education*: https://www.timeshighereducation.com/news/ranking -methodology-2016, accessed December 21, 2015.

31. Răzvan V. Florian," Irreproducibility of the Results of the Shanghai Academic Ranking of World Universities," *Scientometrics*, 72, no. 1 (2007): 25–32.

32. M. Enserink, "Who Ranks the University Rankers?" *Science* 317, no. 5841 (August 2007): 1026–1028.

33. Archambault et al., "Benchmarking Scientific Output in the Social Sciences and Humanities."

34. CWTS Leiden Ranking 2015, http://www.leidenranking.com, accessed December 21, 2015, and http://www.umultirank.org, accessed December 21, 2015.

35. *Maclean's* is a Canadian magazine that annually publishes a ranking of Canadian universities. This citation comes from the newspaper *The Ottawa Citizen*, April 23, 2006.

36. Andrzej Huczynski, *Management Gurus* (London: Routledge, 2006).

37. D. D. Guttenplan, "Questionable Science behind Academic Rankings," *New York Times*, November 15, 2010, accessed December 21, 2015, http://www.nytimes .com/2010/11/15/education/15iht-educLede15.html?pagewanted=all&_r=0.

38. QS Top universities, http://www.topuniversities.com/institution/alexandria -university, accessed December 21, 2015.

39. Mathilde Munos, "Classement de Shanghai des universités: "La France grignote des places" (Fioraso)," *France Info*, August 15, 2013, accessed December 21, 2015, http://www.franceinfo.fr/education-jeunesse/les-invites-de-france-info/classement -de-shanghai-des-universites-la-france-grignote-des-places-fiora.

40. Eleanor S. Abaya, "Marketing Universities Is a Modern-Day Necessity," *University Affairs*, August 5, 2008, accessed December 21, 2015, http://www.universityaffairs .ca/opinion/in-my-opinion/marketing-universities-is-a-modern-day-necessity/.

41. Abaya, "Marketing Universities Is a Modern-Day Necessity."

42. Martin Van der Werf, "Clemson Assails Allegations That It Manipulates 'U.S. News' Rankings," *Chronicle of Higher Education*, June 4, 2009, accessed December 21, 2015, http://chronicle.com/article/Clemson-Assails-Allegations/47295/.

43. Yudhijit Bhattacharjee, "Saudi Universities Offer Cash in Exchange for Academic Prestige," *Science* 334, no. 6061 (December 2011): 1344–1345. See also the many reactions in *Science* 335, March 2, 2012, pp. 1040–1042, and on their website, http://comments.sciencemag.org/content/10.1126/science.334.6061.1344, accessed December 21, 2015.

44. Here, I used the Thomson Reuters "2014 HCR as of September 8, 2015"; see http://highlycited.com, accessed December 21, 2015.

45. Étienne Gless, "Ipag: Les secrets d'une progression 'fulgurante' en recherche," L'Etudiant.fr, October 9, 2014, accessed December 21, 2015, http://www.letudiant .fr/educpros/enquetes/ipag-les-secrets-d-une-progression-fulgurante-en-recherche .html.

46. EFMDP Quality Improvement System, *EQUIS Standards and Criteria*, January 2014, p. 64, accessed December 21, 2015, https://www.efmd.org/images/stories/ efmd/EQUIS/2014/EQUIS_Standards_and_Criteria.pdf.

Conclusion

1. Hans Christian Andersen, "The Emperor's New Clothes," Literature Network, accessed December 21, 2015, http://www.online-literature.com/hans_christian _andersen/967.

2. Sébastien Mosbah-Natanson and Yves Gingras, "The Globalization of Social Sciences? Evidence from a Quantitative Analysis of 30 Years of Production, Collaboration, and Citations in the Social Sciences (1980–2009)," *Current Sociology* 62, no. 5 (September 2014): 626–646.

3. For another useful example of such critical analysis of an impact indicator recently promoted by the National Institutes of Health (NIH), see Ludo Waltman, "NIH's New Citation Metric: A Step Forward in Quantifying Scientific Impact?" November 3, 2015; accessed December 21, 2015, http://www.cwts.nl/blog?article=n -q2u294&title=nihs-new-citation-metric-a-step-forward-in-quantifying-scientific -impact&utm_source=feedburner&utm_medium=twitter&utm_campaign=Feed: +cwts/blog+%28CWTS+Blog%29#sthash.2FkykIIv.dpuf.

Index